Sleeping Dogs

◆

Sleeping Dogs

...Ethics in the Workplace

◆

George Mazzeo

Writers Club Press
San Jose New York Lincoln Shanghai

Sleeping Dogs
...Ethics in the Workplace

Writers Club Press
an imprint of iUniverse.com, Inc.

For information address:
iUniverse.com, Inc.
5220 S 16th, Ste. 200
Lincoln, NE 68512
www.iuniverse.com

ISBN: 0-595-19096-0

Printed in the United States of America

Contents

◆

Introduction

◆

If your morals make you dreary, depend on it, they are wrong.
...Robert Louis Stevenson

To be good is noble: but to show others how to be good is nobler and no trouble.
...Mark Twain

As he often was, Mark Twain was right on this one. It is far easier to formulate theoretical standards of ethical behavior for others than it is to behave ethically ourselves. Let's face it, most of us are amazingly creative at inventing reasons why we believe circumstances make our deviations from the rules both reasonable and necessary. In other words, we are pretty liberal when it comes to granting ourselves a one-time-pass in a moral dilemma. To compound the problem, the more passes we grant, the easier it becomes to grant still another. Before we know it, we can find ourselves pretty far off the high road we intended to travel.

Everyday in our personal and professional lives we are confronted with situations that challenge our ability to choose between right and wrong. Actually, the choice is usually between what is right and what is expedient, with expediency being the far more seductive of the two.

Most of us believe that we have some internal line that we will not cross. The problem is that we are not at all certain where that line is. It moves around depending on the situation; often defined by our level of discomfort with what we are doing.

That's all very interesting, but not particularly useful to a busy professional. What you want are some clear, simple guidelines to steer your actions on a consistent basis in the competitive world you live in. You have a sneaking suspicion (come on, admit it) that always doing the right thing will put you at a professional disadvantage. In an increasingly competitive world it seems that doing whatever it takes is a far better career strategy. I hope to convince you otherwise.

You will find this book sprinkled liberally with quotations from some of the great thinkers of all time (and also some of the most obscure). The consistent message is that the subject of ethics has been an enduring concern of mankind. Over the millennia, men and women have wrestled with the same basic questions about right and wrong and harmony and discord.

The goal of this book is not to moralize or pass judgment. It is not to make you feel badly about yourself or doubt your own character. In fact, my goal is just the opposite, to give you the opportunity to examine the challenges we all face and provide some simple strategies for feeling good about how you resolve them. I plan to keep theory to a minimum and focus on the real world in which we all live. I also hope to make you laugh. Many of the situations we find ourselves in can be quite funny when we step back and view them in the proper perspective. It's all part of our humanity. Here's the bottom line: Fundamentally sound ethical behavior is not only good for the soul, but also a winning career strategy!

Chapter One: Sleeping Dogs

◆

The unexamined life is not worth living.
...Socrates

An over-examined one is worse.
...Anonymous

Most people feel a bit uncomfortable discussing the subject of professional ethics, because they feel uneasy examining their own behavior in too great a detail. Let's face it, the closer you look, the less attractive it gets. Similarly, there isn't much interest in being preached at by some self-righteous theoretician. No one needs any help feeling badly about themselves. With sufficient scrutiny, any of us can find something to feel guilty about all on our own, thank you. If you like sleeping at night, introspection is best taken in small doses. Thinking about ethics can be unsettling and, besides, who has the time? It is much easier to chug along through life doing what you believe necessary than to stop and examine the implications of what you're doing. In the great rat race, it often seems that those rats who pause to examine their actions are the ones who fall behind.

Examined closely enough, almost everything is subject to some ethical criticism. Even getting dressed in the morning can prove to be problematic. Where were these shoes manufactured and under what conditions? Was child or slave labor used? Have I indirectly contributed to some social injustice? Examined in such microscopic detail, every choice becomes an ethical dilemma. If we did this, we would be frozen in a state of indecision and relegated to sleepless nights wracked with guilt. That is not too helpful, nor is it the point. What we are looking for from an examination of professional ethics is a set of simple, universal guidelines that can be applied in our personal and professional lives. Since we don't live in an in an ivory tower, we need practical, real-world solutions.

It's probably safe to assume that most of us don't wake up every morning resolving to do the wrong thing at every opportunity. In fact the odds are that most of us much prefer doing the right thing, although we suspect that sentiment is not shared by our fellow man. We feel pretty good about ourselves, but there is considerable cynicism about the other guy.

As I travel around the country conducting seminars on professional ethics, I always lead off with the following questions. First: How many of you think that there has been a steady decline in moral and ethical standards over the last few decades? Almost 90% answer yes. There is nearly unanimous agreement that the ethical bar has been steadily lowered and actions that might have caused concern in the past now barely register on our collective conscience.

The second question is this: How many of you believe you conduct your personal and professional affairs in an ethical manner? This time the response is even more overwhelming. Ninety-nine percent answer yes. This presents an interesting picture of how we view ourselves, as ethical fish swimming in a polluted pond.

Just how accurate is this view? Is it objective analysis or wishful thinking? Are we applying the same standards to ourselves as we do to everyone else? Exactly what are those standards and who gets to set them? Tough questions all. Let's see if we can work out some answers.

Ethical behavior is not the result of a single event, but rather of a sequence of events, a process. Safety investigators know that accidents don't happen in isolation, but are the product of a chain of discrete actions. Break any link in the chain and the accident never occurs. The same is true of ethical behavior.

There are three components to the ethical process. A breakdown in any one of them can result in an ethical failure. The first required component is ethical consciousness, the second is ethical evaluation, and the third is ethical action. Put another way, you have to know you are in an ethical situation, know the difference between right and wrong, and then have the courage to do the right thing. That sounds simple enough, but of course you know better…or soon will.

*   *   *

You are on a business trip in Los Angeles about to board your return flight to Baltimore when the gate agent announces that your flight is (surprise) overbooked. She goes on to say that anyone willing to surrender their seat will be booked on the next available flight, the "redeye," and be given a free round trip fare anywhere in the system as compensation. Since you and your spouse are planning a vacation in the near future, this is quite an opportunity. You check your day planner and note a meeting at 9AM the following morning with your boss and a prospective new client. That's not a problem. You can sleep on the flight. You'll arrive in plenty of time to go to your apartment and grab a shower and be good to go for the 9 AM. You step forward and surrender your seat.

After killing seven hours wandering around LAX you show up at the gate and board the redeye. Departure time comes and goes and you have not pushed back from the gate. After a while the captain comes on the intercom and announces, "Uh…ladies and gentleman, we are experiencing a slight maintenance problem, but we expect to have things buttoned up and be on our way within 15 minutes." Well, you think, it could be worse. Sure enough, you're right, because in another half-hour the captain comes on again, "Uh…ladies and gentleman, I'm afraid I've got some bad news. Seems that the weather has turned nasty at our destination and is forecast to remain that way for twelve hours. We're going to have to cancel this flight. Please see a gate agent as you exit and we are sorry for any inconvenience."

Well, darn, you think. Guess I'm going to miss that meeting. You take out your cell phone and call the company. It's 2 AM in Boston, so you get the voice mail. You leave a message that your flight has been canceled and apologize for missing the meeting. You say that you'll check in when you get back into town.

You check with the gate agent who tells you that the airline will assist in finding lodging and transportation, but since the flight has been canceled for weather, it will be at your own expense. Not a concern for you, since you are on company time. You grab a cab and head to the hotel. After a few hours sleep you head back to the airport, board your original flight a day late and get into town 24 hours behind schedule.

This scenario usually generates a fair amount of discussion in my seminars, but not right away. The initial reaction is, "nice story…happens all the time…what's the problem?" Perhaps you agree. Many companies allow their business travelers to keep frequent flier bonuses and any other perks that don't cost the company additional money. The fact that you missed your business meeting was just bad luck. You made your decision in good faith. There is no ethical issue here. You're clean on this one, or so you think, but let's look a little closer.

Let's start with the basics. Who is paying for this trip? It's not you, is it? Since you are traveling on the "company dime," don't you think you have an obligation to consider what is best for the company? Yes, you say, but when I made my decision I did not anticipate that there would be any adverse consequences for my employer. Those came about due to unforeseen circumstances. Consider this. Was not your employer, the person paying the bill, entitled to the best possible you at the next day's business meeting? Even had the redeye not been canceled, do you honestly believe that you would have been at your best after a cross-country flight and a shower? Probably not and you probably knew it, but chose to either minimize the impact or ignore it completely.

Now ask yourself this. Who benefited from this decision? This is one of the *Three Critical Questions* to ask yourself as an ethical test of your decision making process. In this case the only possible answer is "me." That should be the first warning flag that you might want to take a second look. Certainly, not all situations where you are the exclusive beneficiary of your own decisions pose ethical problems, but usually such cases are worth another look. The second question is who, if anyone suffers from this decision? In this instance, there was at least potential harm to your employer. So much for the primary issue, now we need to examine your behavior after the flight was canceled.

It appears that you are planning to bill your employer for the room and additional cab fare necessitated by the flight cancellation. Any problem with this? You might be surprised to learn that in every audience, approximately half believe it is perfectly fine to include these fees on their voucher. They can't see any reason why they should incur a financial obligation, since they were traveling on company business. Is it fair to ask your employer to expend funds that were the direct consequence of a decision you made for personal benefit? You are, in effect, asking the company to subsidize a portion of that "free" ticket sitting in your briefcase.

How about the voice mail message you left? It was certainly accurate, your flight had been canceled, but it intentionally stopped short of full disclosure. Was your intent to deceive or to avoid an embarrassing explanation? Was your employer entitled to more? Only you can answer this, because only you know your true intent. There is a big difference between being accurate and being honest and it all has to do with motive and intent.

If something can go wrong, it will.
...Murphy's Law

When philosophers discuss the great ethical thinkers from Socrates to Kant, they often neglect to include that sage of cynicism, Murphy. The truth is, he can't be ignored, because his law applies to an astonishing degree in our everyday lives. His relevance to a discussion of ethics is to highlight the danger of making decisions that seem fine in the short term, but fail to consider possible complications down the road. In general it's best to have a long-range perspective if you want to keep Murphy at bay. Don't look now, but Ole Murph's lurking in the background.

When you get into Baltimore on Friday afternoon it is after business hours, so you head home. Your spouse greets you at the door and says that your boss called and seemed upset. He hadn't supplied any details, but asked that you see him first thing in the morning on Monday. You spend the weekend worrying about what the problem might be. Had there been some difficulty with the new client or was there something else that was troubling him? You know the boss to be a reasonable, even-tempered type who rarely shows his emotions, so something must have been eating at him.

When Monday morning rolls around, you head in early. His car is already in the lot, so you go directly to his office. You knock; he waves you in and motions to a chair. He goes on to explain that the meeting with the prospective new client had not gone well. There were specific questions in your area of expertise that he could not answer. He was sure that the company had lost credibility with the client and that she might be looking elsewhere. You say that you are sorry that you were delayed.

He responds that he was surprised when he had come in Friday morning to get the message that your flight had been canceled and that you would be missing the meeting. You see, he had asked his secretary to check on your flight before leaving the night before and the airline said it had departed on schedule.

You have two choices, try to manufacture a story or come clean. Of course, you realize the only thing you can do now is tell the truth. The boss listens to the details then, in a very direct manner, tells you he is disappointed in your actions and feels you put your personal needs above that of the company's. He asks that you call the prospective client and try to repair the damage. He also says he expects better from you in the future.

This portion of the scenario brings us to the third critical question when testing for ethical correctness. How would you feel if the situation were reversed? Put yourself in your boss' chair and view the events from his perspective. What would you do or say if one of your subordinates had acted in a like manner. Odds are, you would have been equally disappointed.

About that expense voucher, how do you plan to fill it out now? After giving your boss a "severe listening to," there aren't many of us who would be bold enough to charge the additional night's stay and cab fare to the company account. What's changed? The principle hasn't, the facts haven't, only the circumstances have. If it was okay before you knew there was a problem, why shouldn't it be equally acceptable now? Do you suppose that it was never ethical in the first place?

I think you'll admit that there was more to this case than initially met the eye, at least that is what most seminar participants indicate. It is also quite typical. We frequently have ethical lapses simply because we fail to realize that there are ethical considerations involved.

*　　　　　　*　　　　　　*

A lot of people confuse a short memory for a clear conscience.
                                                    ...Doug Larson

Conscience is the inner voice that warns us somebody may be looking.
                                                    ...H.L. Mencken

*One should be more concerned with what his conscience whispers than
with what others shout.*
                                                    ...Anonymous

We all have a conscience, that inner voice that urges us to do the right thing, especially when we really don't want to. As annoying and uncooperative as it can be, it serves as a regulator on our behavior. It is part of our humanity and a required trait to function peacefully within society. We recognize the inherent danger of not having one. In fact we regard the sociopath, someone who seems to have none, as something not quite human, something to be feared.

Although each of us has much in common, we are all programmed differently as a result of our disparate experiences and circumstances. As a result, we react differently in similar situations. We also have differing opinions on the relationship between actions and consequences. Certainly there is a broad range of behaviors into which most of us fit, we call that normal. Anything outside that is considered abnormal and is a hindrance to effectively participating in a society. That being said, even we normal folk diverge on what we believe is the proper behavior in any given situation.

We all struggle to some degree with our conscience. Some of us are extremely hard on ourselves, often setting impossible standards. That's neither healthy nor useful. Others have standards that define the lower limit for acceptable behavior. In fact these folks are constantly testing for the bottom. Their conscience isn't regulated by what they believe is right, but rather by what they think they can get away with. That's what Mencken is referring to in his cynical observation above. Most of the rest of us are somewhere in between.

> *A conscience is like a baby; it has to go to sleep before you can.*
> …Anonymous

A clear conscience is not only required for a good night's sleep, but also to be at peace with ourselves during our waking hours. However, we don't want too much of a good thing. An overly alert conscience can be quite an inconvenience. A good conscience is like a good watchdog, it barks only when you are in danger, but not at every bump in the night. And just as a watchdog eventually becomes attuned to its environment and filters out the routine sounds, so too does our conscience adapt. Gradually and insidiously, events that might have, in the past, set our watchdog to barking, no longer even register.

If you are among the majority who think the ethical bar has been steadily lowered, then this should come as no surprise. If you are in the minority, then all you need do is watch the evening news. Night after night we are bombarded by story after story centered on people in public life who manage to drag the standards down. Instead of being met with public censure, amazingly they continue to thrive.

We see the politician who apparently will say or do anything to keep his office. He is willing sell his principles to the highest bidder or pander to an influential block of voters. He will gladly use the public trust for private gain. The list goes on, but there is little outrage. Why, because we have come to expect it. We dismiss the ethical lapse with the throwaway phrase, "everyone does it." Unfortunately, that not only identifies the problem, but condones it. Except in the most egregious cases, we take no notice. Our internal watchdog is lulled into complacency.

We see the businesswoman who puts her bottom line above everything else. Proudly trumpeting her duty to her shareholders, she misrepresents her product, circumvents regulations and compromises safety. Her company employs an army of attorneys, lobbyists and public relations types to assist in the process. Again, there is no apparent penalty. The message is clear, do whatever it takes. Instead of censure, she is rewarded; and our watchdog's eyelids grow heavy.

We see celebrities of every stripe from the worlds of entertainment and sport parade their lack of character before our eyes to the approval of an idolizing public. Behaviors, once barely tolerable, become commonplace. Once they become acceptable for the prominent, it is no leap at all to see them as appropriate for everyone; and our watchdog is soon asleep.

Never open the door to a lesser evil, for greater ones
invariably slink in after it.
                    ...Baltasar Gracian

It's the old frog-in-the-pan analogy. Drop a frog into a shallow pan of boiling water and he will spring out. Put him in the same pan of water at room temperature, then slowly bring it to a boil and he will make no effort to escape. He adapts to the incremental temperature increase until he eventually dies. As the fabric of our society becomes more and more coarse, we unknowingly do the same thing. We adapt to the incremental lowering of our own standards. The result is often our inability to even recognize we are in a situation where a moral or ethical issue exists. We need to wake the sleeping dogs.

*   *   *

You are the branch manager for a national engineering firm in a large Midwestern city. The branch is programmed for a very large expansion and many people will be transferring in. The corporate policy is to make no public comment on the expansion until the public relations team deems the moment right. To enhance security, the expansion plans have been made known to only a select few on a need-to-know basis. The company considers this to be proprietary information.

One night over a quiet dinner at home with your wife, you casually mention the big news. She is a successful real estate broker and asks that you give her the names of the incoming personnel as they become known. She reminds you that she consistently scores high on customer service questionnaires and that she was recently named citywide Realtor of the year. You know her to be an outstanding professional and that your incoming people would definitely benefit from her services.

You are a little uneasy about providing the names "as they become known" feeling that any contact prior to employee notification and the official announcement of their move would be inappropriate. However, you have no objection to supplying her with the names once the formal announcement is made. She responds that she completely understands and agrees your plan would be more appropriate. You congratulate yourself on having married such a reasonable woman.

This is another case where the overwhelming majority of seminar participants think your actions are appropriate. Most feel that an injunction on divulging proprietary information does not apply between a husband and wife; especially in a relationship of mutual trust. Furthermore, most see no problem with you providing the names at an appropriate time to your Realtor-wife. In fact, many think that since she is such an outstanding professional, you are actually providing a service to your future subordinates. Its all very tidy. Excuse me while I try to rattle the cage and wake up the dogs.

Examined in closer detail this is a case of conflict of interest. Think not? Consider this. How would you feel about a senior defense department official loading up on the stock of a major aircraft manufacturer based on his proprietary knowledge that they would soon be awarded a major government contract? You'd probably say that was unfair and you'd be right. You'd also probably say it was illegal and you'd be right again. Understandably, there are laws that cover conflict of interest cases in government and many other sectors. There is no law that covers your situation, but we are not talking law here. We are talking ethics. Is there a difference in circumstances? Yes, the defense department case involves public office for private gain. The Realtor case is private office for private gain, but the underlying principle is the same.

Let's take a moment to discuss the concept of conflict of interest, since it is central to many ethical dilemmas in professional life. A conflict of interest is a situation where private gain is realized as a product of performing official duties or where professional judgment is, or appears to be, influenced by personal concerns. The result is an unfair advantage and the consequence is a lack of confidence in the objectivity of the official. In matters of confidence, appearances can be every bit as damaging as reality. A professional needs to fastidiously avoid these situations at all times.

How can you do that? A good start is to ask yourself the *Three Critical Questions*: who benefits, who suffers, and what if the situation was reversed? In this case, the beneficiary is your wife by virtue of the expectation of increased clients and income. Since she helps make the payment on the house, the two European luxury sedans in the garage and junior's braces, you are also a beneficiary. Who suffers? Well, you could make the case that her competitors do, but that is a weak argument. In this case she is just networked better. A stronger argument can be made that it is your subordinates who will suffer. You might be putting them in an uncomfortable position. (Did you really want to buy that candy that the boss' kid brought in?) As much as you might stress that they are under no obligation, they may feel otherwise. That's the third question, isn't it? How would you feel if the situation were reversed?

Despite these considerations, you elect to go ahead. It appears to be a good decision. Your wife eventually sells houses to some of the inbound people and not to others. The branch expansion goes smoothly and all is right with the world…at least until Murphy sneaks in the back door.

Six months pass and one of your most experienced division heads is selected for promotion and transfer. You need to promote locally. This is the biggest promotion you can make at your level and is a significant career-advancing move within the company. You are down to two candidates. Maggie, the first, is very talented, but considerably junior to the second candidate, Amanda. Maggie has more potential, but is a little green. Everyone knows she is rising star. Amanda is more experienced, if slightly less creative. Both are capable. It is common knowledge around the coffee bar that these two are the finalists for the big promotion. Everyone is interested in the outcome. You agonize over the decision and eventually come to the conclusion that Amanda would be the best choice. When they moved into town, Amanda bought a house from your wife, Maggie didn't. This is also common knowledge.

Although the fact that Amanda bought a home from your wife never factored into your decision process (at least not consciously), everyone is aware of the circumstances. You made your decision based on your best professional judgment, but you cannot avoid the perception that other considerations influenced the process. These are the types of situations that chip away at the trust between supervisor and subordinate. So, there are not only ethical issues here, but also leadership concerns. A good watchdog might have spared you this problem. The concept of trust is at the heart of any discussion of professional ethics. A strong ethical structure establishes a set of mutual expectations between all parties: superiors, peers, subordinates, vendors, regulators and clients.

As long as we are discussing mutual expectations, it's a good time to clarify an important point. Up until now, we have used the terms morals and ethics interchangeably; it's time to make a distinction. Morality refers to a personal set of beliefs and values. The object of a moral code is to achieve internal harmony, to be at peace with yourself. An ethical code is designed to achieve external harmony. It is a form of social contract among members of society. As such, it requires the agreement and consent of the members of that society. We'll discuss how this consensus is achieved a little later.

*   *   *

> *The worst of all deceptions is self-deception.*
>
> ...Plato

The previous two scenarios dealt with situations where we might not recognize the ethical issues involved. The oversight was not intentional, but rather the result of our lack of sensitivity to the consequences of our actions. Our ethical watchdog had been slumbering. Sometimes, however, our actions are not so innocent. There are times when we intentionally choose to put our watchdog in the closet so that we are not annoyed by his barking. It's just easier to look the other way than it is to confront the problem.

Your company has a clearly defined policy on using the office computers for personal business. It's simple; personal use is prohibited with the exception of sending messages to family members on a limited basis. The policy is firm, unambiguous and widely ignored. You are not a major offender, but do like to forward jokes and email to friends and coworkers. In your opinion there is no cost to your employer and no apparent victim.

One of your coworkers has recently become active in the stock market. He spends an increasing amount of time trading and monitoring his portfolio. He thinks this activity has gone undetected, but you and your other coworkers have taken notice. To this point your boss has not. It is infuriating to all of you that he is tending to personal business for long periods while you are slaving away to meet work requirements. He's a nice guy and there is no compelling evidence that he is not getting his assigned work done, but surely all the time he is devoting to personal finance matters could be put to better use.

You and the others have discussed this situation and are torn between minding your own business and putting a stop to an obvious abuse of company time and equipment.

You have a problem either way in this case. If you elect to do nothing, you must live with the frustration and lack of productivity. This will be a continuing source of annoyance. Since these types of things are cumulative, you can expect your level of discomfort to rise. You can also expect that he will continue to push the limits and may, one day, eventually get caught. The result will be a closer scrutiny of everyone's behavior. Who needs that?

If you confront him, he can point out that what he is doing is no different from what you have been doing, violating company policy. He might even remind you of that joke you sent just the other day. You can make the argument that it is a matter of degree, but a thief who steals $20 is as much a thief as one who steals $20,000. Since it was both convenient and fun to ignore company policy, that is what you chose to do. Every time you wanted to send an unauthorized email, you simply put your watchdog in the closet. Subconsciously, you knew you were wrong, but consciously you gave it no thought at all. It seemed harmless at the time, but in this case an unexpected consequence was that you surrendered the ethical high ground and placed yourself in a weak position to challenge a more egregious offense when it came along.

*   *   *

Your recently unemployed spouse has decided to go into the consulting business. He is working out of your home and trying to keep expenses down, so he occasionally asks you to make some copies or send a fax at the office. You have even run off one hundred copies of his personal brochure using the color copier and high-grade paper. You figure the cost to your employer is minimal when viewed in terms of the overall office operating budget.

He also has his eye on some business software paid for by and licensed to your employer. He asks that you bring the CDs home so he can install them on his personal computer. He points out that since the software has already been paid for, there is no penalty to your employer. There is no victim; no downside and it will save him a large expense. You agree.

This is a typical case of intentionally ignoring the ethical questions involved. You know what you're doing is wrong, but choose do it anyway. It's easier that way! Using company assets for personal use is an abuse of privilege. No matter how minimal you believe the impact, there is an ethical issue here. The same is true with the software. The license grantor has the right to profit from his intellectual property. Your actions circumvent that. This is just a more polite way of saying that in both cases you are stealing. Try the *Three Critical Questions* here. You benefit; your employer and the software manufacturer suffer. Now, reverse it. How would you feel if you were the office manager and came in one day to find an employee running off personal brochures on the copy machine?

The major difference between the first two cases and the last two is your ethical consciousness. You can make the claim in the first two cases that you weren't even aware of the ethical implications. In the latter two, you knew full well that your actions were inappropriate, but chose to ignore the fact. To raise your ethical consciousness, to make your watchdog more vigilant; always ask the *Three Critical Questions*.

However, remember that being aware that there are ethical issues involved is only the first of three links in the required chain to ensure an ethical outcome. You also have to be able to distinguish the difference between the proper and improper course of action and then have the character to actually do the right thing. We'll get to those subjects next. At least for now, we have the dogs awake and barking!

Chapter Two:
Twilight Time

◆

Always do right. This will gratify some people and astonish the rest.
...Mark Twain

The number of people in possession of any criteria for discriminating between good and evil is very small.
...T.S. Eliot

Okay, you've got a problem. The dogs are howling. You recognize that you're are in a situation with ethical implications and you want to do the right thing, but you can't seem to figure out what exactly that is. Unlikely, you think? You have no problem distinguishing right from wrong. Besides, there are plenty of laws to guide your actions and if they aren't sufficient there are always government regulations and company policies. What else could you possibly need?

It's as easy as night and day, you say? You're exactly right and that's the heart of the problem. We all know what night is and we all know what day is, but in which category would you put the period just before dawn and just after sunset? It is neither day nor night, black nor white, but rather somewhere in between…a gray area. The line between the two is blurred. The same thing can happen to the line between right and wrong. Welcome to the ethical twilight time where things are often not as clear as we might wish!

*   *   *

You are on a business trip to Boston in mid-February. It's late after-noon; you have just finished a long day of negotiations. You need to clear your head so you decide to go for a walk. It's almost dark, the sky is slate gray, the temperature is below freezing and the wind is howling. You pull up your collar, shove your hands in your pockets, lean into the wind and press ahead.

You pass over a bridge that spans the Charles River. Midway across, above the whipping of the wind, you hear something that sounds like a cry for help. You stop, look around, but see nothing. You think it must have been your imagination, but then there it is again. You peer over the bridge into the steely water. It's difficult to see, but you continue to hear the cries. Then you see him, a man helplessly flailing and bobbing as the current pulls him down the river! You momentarily make eye contact; it sends a shiver down your spine.

You are an average swimmer at best. You want to help, but jumping in looks like suicide. You are wearing bulky clothes. For all you know the guy is a far better swimmer than you are. You reach for your cell phone, but realize that's not going to help; he'll be long gone by the time any help can arrive. If he is to be saved, only you can do it. What do you do? What are you obligated to do?

Are you morally obligated to put your life at risk to save a stranger? It is only circumstance that brought you to this point. His peril is not of your doing. Most would say of course you aren't. Jumping in would be foolhardy right? Now what? Do you report the incident and identify yourself as the guy who stood by and did nothing while a man drowned? What difference does it make at this point? Is the temptation to just move on?

You don't feel right about that (why not?), so you do dial 911 and report the incident. The police respond, take your statement and thank you for your cooperation. They tell you that you did all you could. That's nice to hear, but how will you be sleeping tonight?

Same bridge, same circumstances, except this time when you look down, it's a woman.

For the male readers, do you feel any differently? Does the fact that it is a woman who is in jeopardy in any way alter the way you view the situation? For the female readers, does it make any difference to you? Let's try it this way. *You* are in the river; do you expect *him* to jump? Would you expect another woman to jump?

When I present this scenario in my seminars almost no one says they would jump in and try to rescue the man. Only about 10% of the men say they would jump in to rescue the woman (so much for chivalry, ladies). The last question is unfair, since anyone in that situation, man or woman, would at least hope that a rescue attempt be made.

Same scenario, but this time it is a small child desperately crying for help.

Now what? It's usually at this point that the number of people who say they will jump starts to increase. The jumpers are still well below 50%, but most of the others are starting to squirm a bit.

You feel a tug at your pant leg. You look down and there is a small boy, perhaps 9 or 10 years old looking up at you with tears pouring down his cheeks. He implores you, "Mister (Lady), please save my sister; can't you see that she's drowning?"

This is getting progressively more difficult? Why? Aren't the principle and circumstance involved the same in each scenario? (Okay, not exactly, as the victim gets lighter and smaller, the odds of a successful rescue go up.) Are you obligated or not? Is a woman's life more valuable than a man's is? Is a child's life of more value than an adult's is? You want to do the right thing, but what is the right thing? It has to be more than a matter of opinion. It is likely that the man's wife; the woman's husband or the child's mother would have a different opinion about what is the correct course of action. Is it really just purely subjective? "I could never just stand there and let someone drown," is an easier opinion to hold when you're not the one peering into the water.

To die for an idea is to place a pretty high price on conjecture.
                                                    ...Anatole France

We are at the second stage of the ethical process, determining right from wrong. We know there is a right thing to do and a wrong thing, we just don't know which is which. Where do we go for guidance? Who decides these things anyway? Fortunately we rarely have to make life and death decisions in our professional lives, but we often find ourselves on a theoretical bridge deciding whether to jump or not. Take the following, all too familiar, case.

*   *   *

Your are a division chief for a mid-size company. The company has been very successful and has gone through a large expansion over the last decade. Many of your subordinates have been part of this tremendous success. As a result you enjoy the support of a loyal and motivated team.

At a senior staff meeting the CEO asks everyone to leave the room except the various vice presidents and division chiefs. "Ladies and Gentleman," he begins, "I'm afraid I have some bad news. The numbers don't look as good as we had hoped. In fact, they are downright frightening. We have expanded too quickly and have been unable to sustain the level of business required to justify current staffing levels. We are losing money at an alarming rate and the quickest fix is to reduce personnel costs. I'm afraid that we have no other choice, but to downsize.

He then turns to you and says that the biggest cuts will come from your division. In fact, you will need to layoff 50% of your staff. You are directed to work with the human resources department to identify the people to be let go. He further states that he realizes your division is finishing up a major contract for an important customer, so the layoffs won't be effective for 180 days. In order to avoid premature departures that might jeopardize the successful completion of the project and possibly undermine the long-term viability of the company, the notification of affected employees is to be delayed for 90 days. Furthermore, there will be no discussion of potential downsizing until the formal announcement is made.

You voice your discomfort with this policy. You feel that the decision should be announced sooner rather than later to allow the affected employees maximum time to seek other employment. The CEO sympathizes with your position, but says that failure of this project could have a disastrous impact on many more people. You have to admit he has a point and reluctantly agree to the plan.

What's the ethical thing to do here? On one hand you want to do right by your subordinates, but on the other hand, the potential of harm to many more is also a real possibility. Like many ethical dilemmas, there are two good answers, but no clear "right" one. The easy way out in this case is to take the I-was-just-following-orders approach, but history tells us that is not always the most ethical course of action.

Over the next two weeks you develop a list of those employees who will be let go. It is based on a combination of performance and seniority. Over coffee one day, Jim, one of the people you have identified for termination mentions to you that he is planning on closing on a new home. His wife is pregnant with their first child and will soon be taking a leave of absence from her job. He's a little nervous, this is his first home purchase and it is a bit of a financial stretch, but he will need the additional room for his expanding family. He's looking for a little moral support and asks you if you think he's making a wise choice. Jim is not only a good employee, but also a good guy; you like him. He's been with the company for three years, but that seniority is way below the cutoff for retention.

Is it ethical to withhold information from an employee that impacts his future? You know that if you tell him the truth, the word is bound to get out with disastrous consequences. The CEO is not likely to be pleased with that. Of course, you could deny being the source of the leak, but that just creates another ethical problem. This is not so different from standing on that bridge trying to decide whether or not to jump. You have to put yourself at risk to "save" someone else.

You could go to the CEO and try to convince him that a full and immediate disclosure is the only right thing to do. If he agrees, your problem is solved. If he doesn't, it is compounded. You are left with three choices: do nothing, leak the information or tell the CEO outright that you can't support the policy and plan to inform your team of the impending layoff. Which would you choose? Before you answer, try to project yourself into this situation. Put aside the fact that you are a detached reader, sitting comfortably somewhere considering a hypothetical situation. Imagine instead that you are in your own office, dealing with your own team members. Need some help? Try the *Three Critical Questions*, especially the third.

> *The most important thing is honesty. Once you learn*
> *to fake that, you're in.*
> ...Samuel Goldwyn

Besides highlighting the difficulty of determining what's right and wrong, this case also raises the issue of the ethical weakness of honesty. That's right, the weakness! Honesty can be a very casual approach to the truth. The term, itself, implies that if asked the right question, you will give the correct answer. This is a very legalistic approach to the truth, more appropriate to a courtroom than our day-to-day lives. The more active approach to the truth is candor: full, unsolicited disclosure.

Suppose you are in the market for a used car. If the vehicle has an oil leak, would you expect the seller to volunteer that information even if you were not astute enough to ask that direct question? Of course you would. You want and expect candor. It is no different in your professional life. So, don't feel too satisfied that you answer all questions honestly, if there is important information being withheld. The difference is clearly intent. Giving an honest answer to a limited question while withholding information with intent to deceive is no virtue.

> *A truth that's told with bad intent*
> *Beats all the lies you can invent.*
> ...William Blake

You haven't made too many mistakes in your brief career as an executive, but one of your biggest was hiring Rick. During the interview process he seemed eager and team oriented. His credentials were exceptional, although he had changed jobs a bit more than normal.

Soon after he started, it became obvious that he had a disruptive attitude. He does not take criticism well and is confrontational with fellow employees. He is certainly competent enough; in fact he's extremely talented. There is certainly no reason to fire him for cause, but he makes each day more of a struggle than necessary. He is one of those people who walk the line; he knows exactly how far he can go short of giving you justification for termination.

You have counseled him on several occasions. He is very defensive and seems to sulk afterwards although his behavior does improve slightly, if briefly. You would love to get rid of him, but can't figure out how.

One day your phone rings, and amazingly enough it is a call from another firm. They are looking to hire Rick and would like your recommendation on his performance. What should you say?

You can be perfectly candid and discuss not only his talents, but also his problems. The result will be that he will not get hired away and continue to be your problem. On the other hand, you can focus on his high talent level and leave the other part unsaid, especially if not asked directly about it. The result of this option might be the answer to your prayers. It's simply a matter of choosing candor over selective honesty. What would you do? Honestly?

*   *   *

Now, back to the question of establishing right and wrong. Throughout recorded history (and no doubt before that) the subject of right and wrong has been a source of considerable intellectual exercise. Starting with the ancient Greeks and continuing to the present day, philosophers, theologians, and the rest of us have wrestled with the concepts of right and wrong, good and evil. Are there some absolute or objective criteria that determine good or is it purely subjective? Before we can establish a set of guidelines for professional conduct, we'll have to answer this question first. Consensus is required if professional ethics is to be a social contract.

To many, this question is no problem at all. They look to religion and secular law to define proper behavior. They believe divine command to be the primary authority, but are prepared to "render unto Caesar" in secular matters as required. Although this seems like a perfectly reasonable approach, it has its shortcomings. There are both philosophical and practical issues to be resolved.

Among the bigger problems with theological-based criteria is that we live in a diverse society. Although there are significant areas of agreement among the major mainstream religions, there is also significant disagreement. Even within these religions themselves, there are differences in interpretation. How do we resolve these conflicts and come up with a standard agreeable to all? What about atheists? What criteria should they use? Surely, there must be some secular standard. Perhaps the law is the answer.

Laws, after all, are put in place by society to ensure fair and equitable treatment for all members of that society and to avoid anarchy. They provide structure and set an expectation of behavior. Isn't that what we want from our ethics? Shouldn't it then stand to reason that if you are in compliance with the law, you are by definition also behaving ethically? On two counts, that is not the case. First, it is possible to have unjust laws and second it is possible to be legal, but unethical.

Laws are a reflection of standards of behavior that are set by those in power. In a dictatorship, that is a single person. In a democratic republic, they are set by elected representatives in conformity with an established constitution. It's easy to see how the former can be flawed, but the latter is also susceptible. Even in a democracy, laws can be merely the codification of what the majority subjectively believes acceptable. It shouldn't be forgotten that for the first one hundred years of our history, slavery was perfectly legal. Sometimes, the most ethical person in a society is the one who stands against an unjust law.

> *To a man with a hammer every problem is a nail.*
> ...Abraham Maslow

Just as engineers frame problems in terms of design and generals in terms of strategy, so too do lawyers see problems in terms of the law. Perhaps it's because laws impact so much of our lives or perhaps because violating a law has a definite consequence, this approach to judging behavior has spilled over into society in general. We are constantly bombarded with images in the media that frame all behavioral issues in terms of what is legal and what is not. It's easy to confuse this with a definition of right and wrong. We constantly hear public officials excuse their behavior by stating that they have done nothing illegal. Our general unease and dissatisfaction with this rationalization tells us that this is not sufficient.

Politicians are forever skirting the law in ways that strain their ethical credibility. Whether it is campaign finance, abuse of power or conflict of interest, they carefully measure their actions against the letter of the law. When challenged, they, and their apologists, are quick to point out that no law has been technically violated. This ridiculous defense is based on the ethically bankrupt theory that if an action is not explicitly proscribed in statute and case law, then it is perfectly acceptable. This is pure nonsense, but it sure seems to sell among the true believers.

Here's a private sector example. No one would argue with a producer's right to make a violent, sexually explicit film. We all agree that this is an issue of freedom of expression that is protected in the United

States by the First Amendment. It is also legal for him to market his product as he sees fit, but is it ethical for him to target his marketing to children? Most would answer no.

Another difficulty with laws (or rules in general) is that if they are worded broadly enough to cover the issue involved, then it leaves large loopholes for wrongdoers to drive through. If they are worded tightly enough to cover specific circumstances, then the wrongdoers just drive around. The result is that is that it's impossible to ever get it exactly right.

There are also questions of equity in the application and enforcement of laws. Recent highly publicized court cases serve to reinforce the common wisdom that the same laws are not applied equally to all people. Wealth, celebrity status, influence, race and many other factors seem to impact the administration of justice. It often appears that if you have enough clever attorneys you can circumvent almost any law. The cumulative effect of all these problems is to diminish the underpinnings of civil law as a foundation for professional ethics. Certainly, every professional realizes that he or she must stay within the law, but they also realize that more is required. Being legal and being ethical are not the same thing. Here's an example that occurs regularly in the professional world.

You run a successful firm with two major projects running simultaneously. Project A is a modest project for a long-time client with whom you have worked many times in the past. You have built a relationship based on mutual respect. Project B is a much larger project for a new, more demanding client. Success on this project will almost certainly mean more business in the future and rapid growth for your company. It's a possible ticket to the big time. The contract for Project A was let before that of Project B.

Here's the problem. Project A is on schedule, but Project B, which is more ambitious than anything you have tried in the past, is falling behind.

You have over-extended your company to work these two projects simulta-
neously and simply do not have any additional resources to apply to
Project B, unless you divert some of the manpower from Project A over to
Project B. Of course, that would mean intentionally delaying Project A.

Your client on Project A has been understanding when delays have
occurred in the past, but you know this particular project is more impor-
tant to him than most. There is no non-performance penalty in your
contract; there has never been a need for one. The client on Project B has
made no secret that he expects his project to come in on time and is not
the easiest person in the world to deal with. He does have a non-per-
formance penalty. He understands that he controls a lot of business and
is not bashful about using this as a "hammer" to get things done how and
when he wants it.

You clearly have the power to bring the second project in on time.
There is no legal impediment. The only thing you will be required to do
is to reallocate the resources, then tell your long-time client that his
project will be delivered behind schedule. Although not legally obligated, you can even offer to make it up to him either financially or in
some other way, but what if he objects?

Typically, I get two answers. The minority opinion is that if Client B
is that difficult, perhaps he isn't the type of person you would want to
deal with in the future, no matter how great the potential rewards.
Besides, you need to value successful, long-term relationships, no matter how modest. The majority disagrees. Their opinion is that this isn't
personal, just standard business practice and considering the size and
structure of the two contracts, you must satisfy the client with the most
leverage.

There is no legal restraint on your action. The law provides no guidance. Does that mean there are no limits on what you elect to do? Do
you see any ethical justification for deliberately delaying a project for

one client at the expense of another? Try the *Three Critical Questions* and see if that helps.

* * *

I know only what is moral is what you feel good after and what is immoral is what you feel bad after.
...Ernest Hemingway

Everyone believes that what suits him is the right thing to do.
...Goethe

Now that we've established that theology and the law are not sufficient bases for establishing a secular professional ethical standard, we need to look elsewhere. Our goal is to determine if there is a more comprehensive and practical standard that we can agree upon. A brief review of some classical approaches to this problem might be helpful.

One classic school of thought, subjectivism, postulates that whether something is right or wrong is simply a matter of opinion. Proponents hold that there is no objective proof of the rightness of any action. So, if someone says that abortion is wrong, they are not really stating anything objective about the procedure itself, but rather expressing their feelings about it. Subjectivists base much of their theory on the fact that if objective criteria actually existed, we wouldn't have such widespread disagreement on such a wide variety of moral issues.

This might be interesting in a purely academic sense, but it is of little use to professionals out there in the real world. If everyone sets their own standard for right and wrong, you have anarchy. Since the purpose of professional ethics is to establish common standards and behavioral expectations within a society, subjectivism is of little value. I mention it only because it leads logically to the next step, cultural subjectivism, which does serve as a basis for ethical standards in many societies.

All fashionable vices pass for virtue.
       ...Moliere

What is morality in any given time or place? It is what the majority then and there happen to like, and immorality is what they dislike.
       ...Alfred North Whitehead

Cannibalism is moral in a cannibal country.
       ...Samuel Butler

Cultural subjectivism is exactly what it sounds like. Right is defined by the prevailing cultural attitude. Under this approach, actions are deemed right when they are in conformity with the majority opinion on the issue. There are still no objective criteria. You can't prove anything, but who cares? Most people feel good about it. Obviously cannibalism is an extreme case, but think about some more interesting examples. In the United States, we take it as a matter of fact that capitalism is the most preferable economic system, but is that something we can prove objectively or is it a matter of cultural subjectivism? How about such divisive issues as abortion, gun control and capital punishment. Should they be decided exclusively by a popularity contest or is something more fundamental at stake? Most of us instinctively believe that there is. Yet, isn't it interesting that proponents on both sides of these issues are constantly citing polling data to reinforce public support for, and by inference the rightness of, their positions?

Do you recall our recent discussion on slavery? Was slavery any more ethical in the first one hundred years of our history than it would be now? The cultural subjectivists would answer yes! They would also answer yes to many things that we find abhorrent (or least fail to understand) in other cultures.

If we look inward, we can see similar problems. How about in your professional life? If the prevailing attitude is that the bottom line is all that matters, is that justification for any behavior that enhances it? In the1980s, the so-called "decade of greed," this seemed frighteningly close to the truth. Cultural subjectivism may serve as a useful tool in developing an ethical code, but for the reasons discussed here can not serve as the exclusive basis.

Wait, you say, something doesn't sound right here. You understand that opinions are subjective, but when you say that it is wrong to steal or to kill an innocent person, you feel you are doing something more profound than merely stating an opinion. It sure feels like you are voicing a fundamental truth. Welcome to the world of moral objectivism.

Philosophy is a search for truth. It is based on starting with the known and then, expanding upon that by the use of reason. The problem has always been where to start. Sometimes, there is no choice other than to start with assumptions. Arguably the most famous of all starting assumptions was René Descartes' *cogito ergo sum*, "I think therefore I am." Moral objectivists also start with an assumption. Theirs is that there are certain fundamental beliefs universally held by all men. The key is "universal," not limited to a particular culture or an individual's status within it. Killing of innocents and stealing are examples of actions that seem to go beyond cultural preferences.

On the positive side, virtues such as integrity, civility, truthfulness, fairness, and compassion are universally accepted (if not always practiced). Unfortunately, adhering to these basic assumptions doesn't help us in every situation. You can be kind, civil and truthful and still not know whether you should jump off that bridge and try to rescue the child who is drowning. You can have integrity and still not know how to handle the privileged information about a coming layoff. So, while you might be off to a good start in developing a code of ethics using moral objectivism, you still need more help.

*　　　　　　*　　　　　　*

The greatest happiness of the greatest number is the foundation of morals and legislation.

...Jeremy Bentham

A school of philosophers in 19th century England, the most famous of whom were Jeremy Bentham and John Stuart Mill, developed an approach to morality based on the outcome of actions. It was called utilitarianism and was based on the theory that an action was right, or most useful, if it produced the greatest number of positive outcomes for the greatest number of people. Right is that which produces the greatest good. This sounds pretty reasonable on the surface and with a few limitations, it is. The major problem with this approach is that it subordinates the rights of the individual. An innocent individual may have to be sacrificed for the greater good.

Our lifeboat only holds 10 and there are 11 survivors; is it ethical to toss the weakest overboard? Most of us would feel uncomfortable with that (although it sure has made a terrific movie plot over the years)! How would you like to be the one explaining to the selected individual, that he (she?) would soon be swimming with the sharks, based on a perfectly reasonable moral philosophy? My guess is that this sort of logic probably plays better in a classroom than in a lifeboat. However, the concept has its place in developing our ethical standards.

Let's try to pull this all together. The foundation of professional ethics begins with the intersection of cultural subjectivism, moral objectivism, utilitarianism and divine command. It's called the Golden Rule. There is some variation of this concept in almost every culture:

What you do not want done to yourself, do not to others.
...Confucius

Whatever you wish that men would do to you, do so to them: this is the law and the prophets.
...Jesus

To do unto all men as you would wish to have done unto you.
...Muhammad

What is hateful to you, do not to your fellow man. That is the entire Law; all the rest is commentary.
...The Talmud

Considering the pervasive popularity of this sentiment across a large and diverse cultural cross section of humanity, we can either conclude that it represents a fundamental truth about the human condition or, at the very least, it is as close to a fundamental truth as we are likely to come. As such, it makes an excellent foundation for our ethical code.

If you are uncomfortable with arriving at this position from a religious/cultural perspective, try Immanuel Kant. Kant was a prolific 18th century German philosopher. He wrote on many subjects to include morality. He was the primary proponent of a school of ethical reasoning known as deontology. His basic premise was that you couldn't judge the morality of an action by its outcome, but rather only by the motive behind it. The sole moral motive is to do one's duty. This seems a bit harsh, since many people perform good acts, not only because they believe it is their duty, but also because they enjoy doing them. The most enduring statement of this philosophy is Kant's Categorical

Imperative: *Act only according to that maxim by which you can at the same time will that it should become a universal law.* Put simply, how would you feel if everybody did this all the time?

Although the Categorical Imperative is not exactly the same as the Golden Rule, it shares a couple of significant similarities. The first is that it is based upon the concept of reciprocal relationships and the second is that it requires you to project yourself into the position of the other parties involved in any situation where ethical issues are in play.

So when building our ethical code, we can start with the idea of reciprocity. To that we add the virtues we discussed previously, such as integrity, civility, truthfulness, fairness, and compassion and we have a good basic structure. We need only add some acceptable standards of good business practice such as respect for intellectual property and the propriety of professional relationships and our framework is complete.

Intellectual property is generally protected by specific prohibitions against passing off someone else's work as your own. Also frequently included are clear rules about post-employment use of proprietary data gained while working for an employer and a prohibition against using that knowledge to lure away clients.

A framework is all we can hope for. We've already established that a comprehensive standard is unachievable. Absolute right and absolute wrong are beyond our comprehension with certainty. That's not a bad thing. What we need and what we have are a set of guidelines that establish a philosophical environment in which we can operate. There is no checklist. We still have to evaluate each set of circumstances and decide on the proper behavior. Even if you are not a member of a profession that has a specific code of ethics, you can still act professionally by following the same guidelines.

I'm sure you have noticed by now that all this analysis leads us back to our simple basic test, the *Three Critical Questions*. "Who benefits?" "Who suffers?" and "What if the situation were reversed?" are really just restating the concept of reciprocity in a series of simple questions.

Imbedded in the first two questions is the utilitarian concept of greatest good. If we ask ourselves these questions and act accordingly, we can feel confident that we are on solid ground for establishing proper behavior in professional situations.

You are the president of a small firm that manufactures fine china. The company is located in a rural section of the Southeast and is the major employer in the small town in which it is located. The local economy rises and falls with the fortunes of the company. It is a very competitive business that depends to a great degree on your reputation for quality. You have labored long and hard to carve your niche in the industry.

One day, your designer comes into your office, closes the door and says, "We may have a problem." It seems that while scanning his trade publications he came across a recent article that identified one of the components of the paint used in your signature trim design as being a potential carcinogen. He double-checked with the supplier who confirmed the presence of the substance in small amounts. The supplier denied any knowledge of a problem with the substance and pointed out that it is unregulated by any agency.

Since the discovery, the designer has done extensive research into the subject and the results are troubling, but inconclusive. It seems that there have been some preliminary studies that indicate that the substance may cause cancer in laboratory rats when administered in large doses. Studies also show that after repeated washings, the substance may begin to leach out of the paint.

Your company has used this paint for the last five years and it is on every piece of china you have sold over that time, well over half a million items. Your designer says that he has found a slightly more expensive substitute paint and recommends you make the switch. You agree. He then recommends that the company make an announcement warning the general public of the hazard. You have a problem with this. You explain that such an announcement is premature based on the available data and the

*potential consequences would be enormous. While you have an obligation
to your customers, you also have an obligation to your employees and the
community. You also point out that the substance is unregulated, so you
feel you have a degree of protection should a problem surface down the
road. "If this stuff were really dangerous," you say, "the government would
be regulating it."*

No matter what business you are in, you have an ethical responsibility to your customers, clients and the general public. An engineer who
designs aircraft components must put the consequences of a design failure above the bottom line. The same holds true in any profession. If you
work in government, where the bottom line is not so large a factor as in
the private sector, you still must consider your stewardship of the public trust. Failure has its consequences. Although your first instincts
might be job preservation, personal gain, or simply convenience, you
must consider the bigger picture.

So, what will you do in this case? Before you answer, I again ask you
to project yourself into the situation. It's easy to take the ethical high
ground when you have nothing at risk. As the president of the company
in this scenario, you have quite a lot at stake.

The issue is whether or not to issue a warning to the general public
and suffer the damage to your reputation and the potential financial lia-
bility for replacing the units. The arguments for keeping silent are that
the research is inconclusive, you will no longer be using the material in
question, and your obligation to your employees and the community. If
the company suffers a catastrophic financial setback, jobs will be lost
and the entire community will suffer. The sole argument for making the
announcement is your responsibility to your customers, but does that
responsibility include a perhaps needless alarm? Can the *Three Critical
Questions* help? Let's see.

Who benefits if you remain silent? The answer is you, your employees and the community. At least that's better than just you! Who suffers?

You can't say for a fact that anyone does. There is the potential, but not the certainty. However, if you do decide to make the announcement, it's certain that there will be negative consequences, and only potential benefits.

Perhaps you are approaching a decision, but you still need to consider the third question. What if the situation was reversed? If you and your family were eating off these plates, would you feel that you deserved notification of the potential danger? You probably would. So, don't your customers deserve the same?

It is difficult to say with certainty that there is a clear right or wrong answer in this case. Kant would disagree and remind you to do your duty, but, as his critics like to point out, he never successfully defined exactly what duty is! No one said this would be easy or that there would always be clear, unambiguous answers. The point of this case study, as with all of them, is to raise your ethical consciousness and get you thinking about actions and consequences.

*   *   *

Do you have enough to think about yet? Well, here's something else to consider. Even if you have agreement on the ethical principle involved, you still can have disagreement on the proper course of action. That's because each ethical puzzle has two distinct pieces. There is a principle piece and a factual piece.

Take the issue of abortion. In the United States you can find broad agreement on the statement: It is wrong to take an innocent human life. We have near consensus on the principle involved. However, there remains significant debate on the facts. Specifically, at what point does a fetus become a human being? The result is a great national divide on this emotional issue.

The problem can also be reversed. Take the issue of capital punish-ment. Webster defines murder as the unlawful, premeditated killing of one human being by another. There is broad consensus on the fact of what constitutes murder, but not so on the ethical principle involved with capital punishment. Opponents say that murder is murder and, therefore, capital punishment is unjustified. Nonsense, argue the pro-ponents; it's perfectly ethical. The punishment should fit the crime. Besides, argue the utilitarians, it serves the greater good as a deterrent to others.

There are many similar issues in the professional world. For instance we can agree on the ethical principle that accepting a bribe is wrong. However, the factual definition of bribery is more of a problem. What constitutes a bribe? Is it defined by a dollar amount or value (the gov-ernment and many companies think so), or is about motive. Does the benefactor expect a *quid pro quo* from the beneficiary? Does giving a gift or picking up the tab for lunch qualify? One thing is for sure; doing the right thing is quite a bit harder than it appears.

*   *   *

So far we have been operating on the assumption that we first estab-lish a set of ethical standards, then as situations arise we apply those principles to determine the correct course of action. Sometimes, that process can get reversed. We call this reversal situational ethics; it is a case of putting the cart before the horse. We assess a situation, then decide which ethical principle should apply.

You work on a design team for a software provider. Your team is in the process of developing a major new business application that has enormous upside potential in a very competitive market. Due to an impending departure, the team leader position will soon become vacant. You would love to get this promotion, but realize that you are probably too junior to be a serious contender, especially with so many talented people to choose from.

After a round of preliminary interviews, it becomes the world's worst kept secret that the field has been narrowed down to three contenders, all current team members. You aren't one of them. There is considerable anticipation and speculation among the rest of the team as the process nears completion. The importance of the upcoming project and the need for solid leadership is of natural interest to all. You think highly of all the candidates and really don't have a preference. You just want the decision to be made so the team can concentrate on the task at hand.

One day as you are having a cup of coffee in the break room, Jen, one of the finalists, sits down next to you. You have been coworkers for a few years and have a cordial relationship. You ask, conversationally, how she's holding up under the pressure of the selection process. She answers that she is doing just fine and that while she would obviously like the promotion, it isn't the focal point of her life right now. "Don't tell anyone, but I have some wonderful news. I'm pregnant." She goes on to say that she isn't sure what she will do after the baby is born and may even take a leave of absence or resign outright.

You are uncomfortable with this information and curse the fact that you are one of those people who others feel comfortable opening up to. You are happy for Jen, but concerned about your team. The timeline for the project is 18 months and that is probably optimistic. There are a lot of stakeholders in the process and it will require considerable negotiation and coordination. You feel continuity of leadership will be critical to success.

You are pretty sure the division chief is unaware of the situation. Of course, even if she was, it would be illegal for her to factor that into the promotion decision, nor would you ask her to. Still, in such a close competition, it might make a difference on some unconscious level. You don't have a horse in this race and have nothing against Jen, but feel that *in the interest of continuity, it would be better if one of the other two candidates were chosen. You decide that you will find some way to casually leak the news of the pregnancy to the division chief.*

One of the basic principles in every established professional code of ethics is an admonition against providing information potentially damaging to a colleague or competitor. The underlying principle is sound. A professional should succeed or fail based on their performance, not on the manipulation of information by a third party. Failure to adhere to this principle creates an atmosphere of distrust, a politically charged work environment, and diminishes teamwork and morale.

The ethical decision making process has been reversed here. The correct sequence would have been to enter the process with a firm set of ethical standards, in this case to not provide damaging information, and then to apply them to the situation. If you had done that, you would have kept the pregnancy information to yourself. You reversed the process, evaluating the situation and then deciding what the principle should be, in this case (at least in your opinion) the good of the team. Sounds noble enough, but it is playing fast and loose with ethical standards. This process reversal is symptomatic of situational ethics.

Although the term carries a negative connotation, the concept is not without redeeming value. The folks who coined the phrase in the 1960's were looking for a middle ground between the extremes of anarchy and legalism. There is some merit to the idea that there are very few moral absolutes that apply in all situations. The danger is that, when carried to extremes, it provides justification for too wide a range of behaviors. This is a legitimate cause for concern. Here's another example.

You are the human resources director for a manufacturing firm. The company has always been a drug free workplace that requires employees to sign a consent form for drug testing after any injury-related safety incident. The board has recently decided to take the program to the next level and require drug screening prior to employment.

You have been a recreational marijuana user since college. Since the chances of an injury related accident occurring in the HR office were infinitesimal, you never felt threatened by the existing policy and since all current employees will be grand-fathered when the new policy goes into effect, that is no threat either. You have no problem administering the policy even though you think it is too broad and too intrusive.

You can understand why equipment operators, drivers and others need to be drug free, since the potential for injury is great. You also understand that the company can't have separate standards for different categories of employees, but you have no intention of changing your habits. Your action is hurting no one.

The problem here should be evident. You are not operating from an existing principle, but rather are assessing the situation and then deciding what you think the operative principle ought to be. You see your situation as different from that of other employees and therefore measure yourself against different criteria. You are displaying situational ethics.

*   *   *

As previously mentioned, a key element of professional ethics is a respect for intellectual property. There are legal injunctions against plagiarism, but many ethical lapses fall well below that standard. Taking credit for another person's work or idea is dishonest. It attributes to the offender a creativity or skill that he does not posses or has not demonstrated. For example, an engineer can't pass off someone else's design as her own. There are similar examples in all professions. Taking credit for someone else's work demonstrates a lack of integrity and undermines trust in the work place.

You work on the marketing team for a sporting goods firm. Your company focuses on high end, trendy sports apparel. You and your team have been asked to develop ways to effectively promote your products in the college market.

One night while working late, you and an associate are sharing a pizza and doing a little brainstorming. Your associate says, "You know, I think we might have the answer right here in front of us. I know it sounds crazy, but we ought to advertise on pizza boxes. Think about it. What college kid doesn't eat pizza? We just need to target the pizza joints adjacent to university campuses and attach flyers. Maybe we could even partner with them to offer discounted pizza. What do you think?" You think that the plan is crazy and don't offer much support.

Two weeks later at the marketing staff meeting, the director says that the CEO is tired of the same old marketing suggestions and wants some outside-the-box (no pun intended) thinking. He looks around the room and says, "Any ideas." Your coworker is away on business, so you say, "You know, it may sound crazy," and lay out the pizza box idea. You conveniently fail to mention this was someone else's idea. The director loves it; he passes it on to the CEO who also loves it and comments on your creativity and potential. You graciously accept the accolades.

You are accepting credit for an idea that is not your own. This action fails the *Three Critical Questions* test in a very large way. The result will be a poisoned relationship with your coworker and when the word gets out (as it most certainly will) a loss of respect and trust among all your team members. This problem here is obvious, but there are circumstances where it can be subtler.

You are a headhunter for a major executive search company. A number of your clients have been particularly pleased with your work and have suggested you go out on your own. After much soul searching you decide to give it a try. You know from your association with current clients that they have numerous positions still unfilled, but have not yet contracted with your current employer to fill them. You also have a long list of prospective candidates that you developed while trying to fill the current positions. Many of these will be an excellent fit for the remaining vacancies.

You give notice to your employer and announce to your clients that your professional services are now available. You secure a number of contracts and fill the positions with candidates off your exiting list. Life is good.

Many professionals have a non-compete clause in their contracts, but even without a legal restriction, there are often ethical concerns. It is generally considered unethical to use information gained in the employ of another to compete with them at a later date. In the case above, remember that the candidate list was developed while on salary for your former employer. He could make a pretty good case that it is his property.

Before we go overboard, let's make something clear. Rarely does an individual go into business on their own without taking his or her Rolodex with them and there is nothing unethical about it. He or she is also very likely to seek business from clients with whom they have an established relationship. There is nothing unethical with that either. It's only when they use employer or client-specific information gained in the employ of another that they cross the line.

Chapter Three:
The Ethical Gymnast

◆

We lie loudest when we lie to ourselves.
...Eric Hoffer

We began our discussion by stating that an ethical behavior is the result of a three-step process. The first step is consciousness, realizing there is an ethical issue at stake. The second is evaluation, being able to distinguish between right and wrong. The final step is having the requisite character to actually do the right thing. Many of us have a problem with this final step, because the right thing is not always convenient.

The choice usually boils down to doing what is right or what is expedient. The problem is that the expedient course of action can be so very tantalizing. It calls to us with its siren's song of instant gratification. If we know anything about modern society, it is our overwhelming desire for instant gratification. We are impatient by nature and by culture. We tend to have a very shortsighted view on the consequences of our actions.

This presents us with a dilemma, we know the right thing to do, but really don't want to do it. The problem is, we don't want the watchdogs of our conscience barking at us. We need to mollify or distract them so that they don't keep us awake at night. The sociopath has no problem here, he doesn't own any dogs, but the average person does. We don't like to see ourselves as self-serving or amoral, so we construct excuses for our behavior. Sometimes, this requires us to do some very imaginative ethical gymnastics as we fashion the tortured logic to justify our transgressions. Some of the examples we will soon discuss will illustrate the gold medal-wining form we use to craft our justifications. These excuses are meant for private rather than public consumption. In fact when trapped and forced to verbalize them, we are often embarrassed at the shallowness of our own argument.

> *Man is the only animal that blushes. Or needs to.*
> *...Mark Twain*

This process of self-deception is called rationalization. Webster handles it this way: to devise superficial, or plausible, explanations or excuses for one's acts, beliefs, or desires, usually without being aware that these are not the real motives. In other words, a process of deliberate self-deception to justify something that otherwise is unjustifiable. That sounds sinister...and it is! It is indicative of a weak character and a willingness to compromise principle for profit.

> *Don't part company with your ideals. They are anchors in a storm.*
> *...Arnold Glasgow*

> *Our character is what we do when we think no one is looking.*
> *...H. Jackson Browne*

When we come to an ethical decision point, we often grant ourselves a one-time pass to ignore the facts and principles and to proceed as we desire. There are two problems with this approach. The first is obvious; we have compromised our values. The second, and perhaps more dangerous, is the cumulative effect. The more we make such decisions and appear to suffer no consequences, the more that behavior is reinforced. It becomes easier and easier to make further rationalizations. The result is an insidious and relentless erosion of our moral and ethical foundations. Before we know it, those self-awarded passes become the new standard for our behavior. Our ethical bar has been lowered.

Rationalization has become an art form. We devise many an ingenious excuse for our behavior, even to the point of convincing ourselves that we are actually doing something noble. Our deviation from our ethical standards is done, not for personal gain, but rather for the good of all (well, most anyway) concerned. Darn, we're good! Let's check with the judges. Yes! A perfect 10!

It would be impossible to list all the rationalization approaches, because we are just so darn good at inventing new ones. However, we can discuss some of the more common ones, try point out the weakness of the logic, and give you the opportunity to see if you recognize any similar behaviors in your colleagues (easy) or yourself (a bit harder).

You are a mid-level executive with a large retailer that has a strict policy on fraternization. It forbids dating between a supervisor and subordinate. Despite this clearly defined policy (it's right there in the employee handbook), you have become involved with one of your subordinates. In your opinion, the company policy is too intrusive. They have no business meddling in your personal life. You are both mature, single adults and see no reason why you should be prohibited from dating. In these highly competitive times, you find that you spend most of your life at work. When and where would you even have the opportunity to meet anyone else?

You have been very discreet, but lately you both have gotten the impression that your coworkers might be aware of the relationship. No one has said anything, but you have noticed a few sly smiles from others whenever you are together, and on occasion conversation has stopped when you have approached a group. Perhaps you are just being paranoid.

You knew and agreed to the rules as a condition of employment and yet are ignoring one of them. Worse yet, you are in a supervisory position where you are responsible for enforcing policy. You rationalize this by attacking the legitimacy of the policy itself. This is known as the moral override argument. Since the rule is unjust, I am not obliged to adhere to it.

This argument has some merit. History has shown us that sometimes the most ethical position to take is the one in opposition to the existing law. Most would agree that those opposed to slavery in the first one hundred years of our history held the moral high ground as did the opponents to the regime in Nazi Germany, but don't be too quick put yourself in that company.

The people in opposition to an immoral law do not personally benefit from that opposition, but rather are motivated solely by principle. They are not excusing themselves based on convenience; in fact, the opposite is usually true. Their opposition puts them at risk. You have another problem here. By virtue of your supervisory position you are charged with enforcing policies. This is difficult to do selectively. If you are known to be in violation of one policy with which you might happen to disagree, it undermines your moral authority to enforce every other policy. How can you rationalize your right to pick and choose without acknowledging the same prerogative for everyone?

I once worked in the public sector for a very rigid, by-the-book boss who was notoriously tough on his subordinates. He demanded strict adherence to all government regulations. He was a very senior official and apparently felt he could excuse himself from those regulations that were inconvenient for him. He was a notorious chain smoker and smoking was prohibited by regulation in government vehicles and offices. This was inconvenient, so he ignored it. He smoked in his government vehicle and when traveling on government aircraft. Worse yet, he would smoke in his office. He would keep a lit cigarette in an ashtray in his upper right hand desk drawer. The result was a predictable loss of moral authority. He still had the legal authority vested in his powerful position and was apparently satisfied with that, but any reference to the need to stick to the rules just exposed the hypocrisy and undermined his ability to lead.

Here's another consideration. Can you be absolutely certain that your opinion is ethically correct or is it merely a personal preference? Does the possibility exist that you have incomplete knowledge of the issue? Is it possible that the rule-makers have a broader perspective or have greater experience with these type situations? It takes a certain amount of arrogance not to admit that this is not, at least, a possibility. Have you considered the long-term implications or that Murphy may be lurking down the road?

It is three months later and the relationship is still going strong to no one's detriment. Obviously there is no victim and your judgment has been vindicated. You are now quite sure that at least some of your coworkers are aware of the situation, but there has been no direct acknowledgment or adverse effect.

One day your boss calls you into the office. He says that a supervisory position similar to yours is opening up in another division. He has decided to fill the vacancy from your staff and has narrowed the search to two candidates, but can't completely make up his mind and wants your recommendation. He feels that since you work most directly with them, you are in the best position to decide and that your recommendation will be the tiebreaker. One of the candidates, the one

*you honestly feel is best qualified and most deserving, is your partner in
the relationship. What do you do?*

Perhaps that policy wasn't so shortsighted and intrusive as you
thought. You are now in a no-win situation. If you select your partner,
no matter how well qualified, you will be creating the impression that
there was more involved than just job performance. The result will be a
loss of trust in your judgment and a corresponding reduction in your
ability to lead. If, on the other hand, you elect to choose the less qualified candidate to avoid the appearance of partiality, you are penalizing
your partner and not acting in the best interest of the company.

If you choose the latter, you better have a very good relationship,
because if your partner becomes disgruntled and suggests that there was
a *quid pro quo* implied in the relationship, you are vulnerable to an accu-
sation of sexual harassment. Your convenient self-deception based on a
moral override has turned out to be just a dangerous rationalization.

Here's an interesting side bar to this scenario. Who do you think is
more culpable, the supervisor or the subordinate? Perhaps you think they
are equally at fault, after all, they were both subject to the same policy. On
closer examination, most agree that the supervisor is more culpable, by
virtue of his or her leadership responsibilities, and certainly more vulnerable to harassment charges. The supervisor can't claim coercion or fear of
repercussion, but the subordinate sure can. Do you think the subordinate
automatically surrendered the expectation of equal consideration when
he or she entered into the relationship? If so, do you think they under-
stood that when they began the relationship? Me neither.

*   *   *

What's in name? A rose by any other name would smell as sweet.
                              ...William Shakespeare

...but would not cost half as much during the wintertime.
                              ...George Ade

You are a purchasing agent. At a trade show, you run into a salesman for one of your major vendors. You frequently use his company and a few others to supply common components for the office furniture you manufacture. He's is in constant competition with your other vendors. The small talk turns to holiday plans and you mention that you sure could use a break from this Chicago winter and that you were considering a trip to Southern California.

The sales rep replies that his boss owns a houseboat that he keeps anchored in San Diego. He doesn't get a chance to go down as often as he would like and feels that the extended periods of disuse are not good for the boat's systems. Fearing damage and misuse, he doesn't like to rent to strangers. He prefers friends or others that come highly recommended and gives them an excellent rate. You say you are interested and the rep promises to get back to you.

The next day, you get a call. The sales rep says his boss is delighted to hear you might be interested. Since you are doing him a big favor, he will make the boat available for the nominal fee of $100 a week. The boat houses 6 comfortably and has all the amenities. You jump at the opportunity.

There is no mention of a quid pro quo and there is no gift involved. So, no problem either, right? Not so fast, let's take a closer look. You are being offered a benefit at a cost substantially below fair-market value from a vendor who has a vested interest in currying your favor. As a purchasing agent, you decide who gets your company's business. As such, agreeing to this arrangement is a conflict of interest. You are accepting a benefit that could effect your objectivity in deciding among competing vendors.

Too harsh you say? How can this be viewed as a bribe or gift when you are the one paying? Besides, the reason given for the favorable rate makes perfect sense. You are doing the man a favor. No one has asked for special consideration in future dealings, so there is no linkage between the rental and your professional duties. This is simply a mutually beneficial private arrangement, completely separate from any professional interests. That sounds good, feels good and is completely wrong. A bribe is a bribe. A gift is a gift. A conflict of interest is a conflict of interest no matter what you choose to call it. If it walks like a duck and quacks like a duck, there's a good chance it's a duck!

> We do what we must and call it by the best names.
> …Ralph Waldo Emerson

This type of rationalization is called creative labeling. We don't want to call a spade a spade so we call it something else. It's easier that way. This case seems pretty harmless, but it is closely related to a number of issues that are troubling in today's society. No one goes around calling him or herself a terrorist; no, they are a freedom fighter. You're not lying; you are merely interpreting the data to make the most favorable case for your product or service. You're not a political spin-doctor; you're an advocate. How we choose to label what we do speaks volumes about our character.

From an ethical perspective, it doesn't matter what we say. What matters are our actions and intentions. How many times in your business dealings have you seen the selective use of statistics used to enhance the actual performance of a product or service? The person who manipulates the statistics knows that, while the individual datum may be correct, the picture being painted is intentionally inaccurate. That's not lying, right? It's favorable advertising. If the intent is to deceive, it is a lie. Changing the label does not change the action or the character of the actor.

If you reflect on your own career, you can no doubt think of at least a few instances where you have tried to put a sunny label on a cloudy action. It's natural for us to try to feel good about what we do. That's what makes creative labeling so attractive and, as a consequence, so dangerous. We know our actions are wrong, but to avoid having to deal with these homely relations, we dress them up in fancy outfits and parade them around as the family beauties.

*   *   *

A vendor is sponsoring a free seminar in your city focusing on compliance with government environmental regulations. Information will be provided on a new process to filter regulated substances from smokestack emissions. The vendor is on the leading edge of this technology. The all-day seminar will include lunch and a social hour afterwards where hors d'ouevres and drinks will be served. You are responsible for EPA compliance at your firm and accept the invitation to attend.

Do you see a problem here? No? Me neither! Okay, I threw this scenario in to make sure we haven't lost our perspective. When you get involved in discussions about ethics, you can fall into the habit of seeing demons everywhere. In a purely academic environment, we can be too quick to find fault where none exists.

In this case, it is a common and accepted business practice to put together a seminar to inform potential clients about a product or service. These seminars provide a valuable educational service. The vendor is able to get his capabilities out to the public. All parties benefit. A meal and a drink are hardly excessive and therefore not likely to serve as a basis for a quid pro quo. Now, if the seminar was in Maui and room and airfare were provided, that would be a different case!

*   *   *

Beware of the half-truth. You may have gotten hold of the wrong half.
...Anonymous

You are the manager of the information technology department for a thriving law firm. The partners have decided to purchase new, state-of-the-art, laptop computers for all the attorneys on staff. At the meeting where this was decided you advocated that additional units be purchased for the senior, non-attorney staff members such as yourself, but were unsuccessful in convincing the partners who felt that the potential productivity gains did not warrant the additional expense. They felt that the limited travel schedule of the non-attorneys did not justify the need for a laptop. You are disappointed because as a "techie" you really wanted to get your hands on one of the new computers, but you acknowledge to yourself that your case was weak.

After a careful market search, you decide on the machines that you wish to purchase and place an order for 30 units. When the order arrives you are surprised to note that 31 units have been delivered. You check the invoice, and sure enough, you have only been billed for 30. You consider the alternatives and decide to keep the extra machine for your professional use.

Here's how you see it. You plan to use it only for company business. There is no down side. Having access to the machine will allow you to become more familiar with the equipment. As a result, you will be in a better position to provide advice and service to the attorneys you support. Additionally, should there be a problem with one of their machines, you will have a "loaner" ready to go. All this additional benefit comes at no cost to the firm. It's not like you took the thing home for personal use.

You instinctively know something is wrong with the rationale here. Obviously, your firm is getting something that hasn't been paid for. You know that isn't fair. Before you dismiss this case out of hand, I suggest you reflect on your personal experience. How many times have you done something you knew was at least slightly unethical, but rationalized it away on the basis that it could have been worse or that others have done far worse? This type of rationalization is known as fault ranking.

It is a common defense offered by offenders after they are caught. In an attempt to put the legal or ethical transgression in, what the offender feels to be, the proper perspective, he or she will point to more egregious examples. This is a favorite tactic used by politicians who, when cornered, will trot out every historical ethical lapse that trumps their own.

A recent incident in college athletics illustrates my point. A star football player at a major university was caught on film in a minor scam involving a retail clerk. He had been purchasing clothes at a department store for ten cents on the dollar with the complicity of the clerk. When finally caught he apologized, but added, "It's not like I shot the President." In other words, sure I was wrong, but it's not that big a deal.

There are several problems with this approach. First, wrong is wrong, quibbling over the magnitude of the transgression is hardly a defense. Second, unless carefully constructed, most analogies are imperfect and you end up comparing apples and oranges. Differing situations and circumstances affect the comparisons. Third, you are not declaring your innocence, but rather pointing out that you could have done worse. Stipulating that you are capable of worse is not exactly staking out the moral high ground, is it?

In the case of the laptop computer the *Three Critical Questions* provide some insight. Who benefits? The idea that this is a benefit to the firm is a story woven out of whole cloth. Who suffers? You say no one, since it is at no additional cost to the firm, but you know full well that the supplier is the victim. If the situation was reversed, and you were the supplier, would you not want to be reimbursed for the product or have the machine returned? So, even though you are correct in stating it could have been worse, that isn't justification, it's rationalization by fault ranking.

*   *   *

You work in the claims office of a medical insurer. Your team is charged with tracking and analyzing customer satisfaction data. You are responsible for putting together the semiannual report to the board of directors. Your company has recently undergone a major reorganization with the specific goal of turning around a customer satisfaction rate well below industry standards.

Poor customer satisfaction has resulted in mass client defections and a rapidly declining market share. The loss of revenue has put the company in a difficult cash-flow position and future viability is by no means guaranteed. The good news is that the most recent data indicate the problem may be turning around. For the last three months the trend in customer satisfaction has been up. Unfortunately, the final two of those months fall outside the established period of the report, so it will not accurately reflect the turnaround.

This particular report is of great significance, because a "white knight" has appeared and is prepared to make an offer on the company, if the reorganization proves successful. Your report will go a long way in establishing whether that has happened or not. The sale would mean an infusion of capital and would ensure the firm's survival.

You and your boss, the customer service director, are kicking this problem around when she astounds you with the following proposal. "Look, you and I both know that the recent management initiatives are beginning to work and that all the indications in the customer service arena are good. The period of this report is just an arbitrary slice of the calendar. I'd like you to drop off the first two months of the reporting period and replace the data with the most recent two months. All we are doing is sliding the six-month window forward to more accurately reflect what is happening in the marketplace."

You are more than a little uncomfortable with this and say so. Your supervisor looks you in the eye and says, "Perhaps you misunderstood what I said to be a request, it wasn't. Please prepare the report as directed and have it on my desk by Friday. I always thought you were a team player, don't disappoint me now." You prepare the report as requested.

It is not uncommon to find yourself in some variation of this dilemma, being asked or directed to do something that you feel uncomfortable with from an ethical perspective. In fact, I'd be surprised if any of you haven't been there and done that. This is another one of those cases that seems clear enough in an academic situation, but is considerably messier in real life. There are a number of difficult considerations.

First, everyone wants to be considered a team player; your boss pushed the right button there. The consequences of the sale not going through could be dire not only for you, but also your coworkers. There is no sense of proportionality. On one hand you have only your personal discomfort, while on the other the good of your organization and all the people in it. The utilitarian in you is inclined to justify your action based solely on that. From that perspective, what's a little discomfort anyway? Then you have the problem of incurring the wrath of your boss. Once again, your job could be at stake. The survivor in you (and the realist) is inclined to cooperate. Besides, you have the perfect excuse should you get caught. I was just doing what I was told.

Nice try! This rationalization is called fault reassignment. The evil deed is not your fault; it's somebody else's. This rationalization usually takes one of two forms. The first is the I-was-just-following-orders approach. This is a morally bankrupt position. It didn't work as a defense for Nazi war criminals and it won't work for you. Even the most structured segment of our society, the military, recognizes the fact that an order must be moral and legal before it must be obeyed. You cannot dodge ethical obligations by citing misguided notions of duty.

Well, you say, thanks for the lecture, but what am I supposed to do when confronted with this type of situation? I have a family to support and a career to worry about. The view might be pleasant from the ethical high ground, but it can be a lonely and a hungry place. There are a few things you might try. First, you can make the case as forcibly as possible that you think "fudging" the data is wrong. You might also propose an alternative, possibly an addendum to the report that includes the optimistic data, but what if that fails?

> *Expedients are for the hour, but principles are for the ages.*
> ...Henry Ward Beecher

Taking the long-term view of an ethical dilemma often reveals the best solution. Sure, you could surrender your principles and get through this particular problem. That would certainly be expedient, however, there is also a downside. Once you have demonstrated that you will compromise your integrity under pressure, there is a greater likelihood you will be asked to do so again. Be prepared to be uncomfortable on a regular basis. It's a slippery slope. On the other hand, if you resist, you are unlikely to be approached again. As a practical matter, you might mention that you plan to draft a memorandum for record that you refused to comply with your boss' orders. This might make things unpleasant, but it will also serve to protect your position. Depending on the degree of unpleasantness, it might be time to start looking elsewhere.

You also have to ask yourself how much you want to work for a person who would ask you to do something unethical. Will you be able to trust her in the future? Will you always have to wonder if she is being honest with you? Will she be withholding information or hiding her real motives? Even if you decide to go along, you probably need to be looking for other opportunities. Since the long-term results are likely to be the same, namely you seeking other employment, you might as well make the ethical choice.

Here's an important point. One of the fundamental purposes of professional ethics is to establish trust in the work environment. When any party chooses to breach the ethical standard, that trust is destroyed. In the long term that can only have a detrimental effect on professional relationships, morale, and eventually the bottom line. That is why what appears to be expedient in the short-term is usually counterproductive in the long-term.

The second form of fault reassignment is the blame-the-victim approach. This construction puts the responsibility for our actions on the person who suffers the consequences. For instance, a man accused of sexual harassment might try to justify his behavior by accusing his victim of acting or dressing provocatively or sending mixed signals. It's not his fault; it's hers. Using the same rationale an embezzler tells himself that if his employer would only pay him a decent wage, he wouldn't need to be taking company funds. There are many similar cases in our professional and personal lives where we try to justify unethical behavior by assigning blame elsewhere. The problem is, it just won't wash.

You are responsible for your actions. No matter what the perceived provocation, you are obligated to adhere to your ethical standards. To do otherwise is simply another form of situational ethics. Your mother told you that two wrongs don't make a right. You should listen to mom.

*   *   *

You are the chief financial officer for a leading toy manufacturer. Your company is the subject of a lawsuit alleging that, despite prior knowledge of a potential safety defect, it continued to aggressively market a new toy. A child has suffered an eye injury using your product. A senior staff meeting is called with counsel present to develop a strategy for dealing with the litigation.

The lawyers lay out the case. It has two parts. The first is relatively simple. They will try to minimize the impact of the damages and negotiate compensation for the victim if necessary. They will point to the firm's outstanding safety record and the socially responsible way the product was reengineered when the problem was identified.

The second issue is the bigger problem. If the company had prior knowledge of a safety defect and failed to recall it, you will be liable for much greater damages and suffer a public relations disaster. The question is what did you know and when? The lawyers excuse themselves from the meeting and leave the staff to reconstruct the events.

The president asks the chief engineer to summarize the product development history. She responds that, as always, rigorous design criteria were used to make the product as safe as possible. She reminds everyone that nothing can be made completely child proof, because children are such clever devils. Prototypes were built and sent to an independent agency for testing. The results were positive and she has the documentation to support it. So much for the good news.

After the product was put into mass production, the firm received a handful of non-injury complaints that a spring was popping loose rendering the toy inoperative. An engineering analysis showed that under certain circumstances the failure could be duplicated in the lab. More troubling, the report indicated that in a few very extreme circumstances, the spring came loose with sufficient force to cause injury, especially to the face. The report was very clear on this point: the conditions that caused this type of spring ejection were so extreme that the likelihood of it happening was infinitesimal. Using this report, the design was changed and there have been no subsequent failures.

She further reminds everyone that the staff was briefed on the facts over a year ago. At that meeting the issue of whether or not to recall the units already on the market was discussed. Being extremely conservative, she recommended a recall or at least further research. The majority opinion was that since the possibility of an injury-related failure was remote, a recall was unnecessary. Further research would serve no purpose and could possibly endanger plausible deniability. As director of marketing, you supported the decision. The chief of engineering was the only dissenting opinion.

The president solicits further comment, then summarizes the inputs. He states that the position of the firm will be that there was no prior knowledge of a safety defect. A design defect existed and was corrected, but the defect related to the operation of the toy, not its safety. Since all toys that were returned to the company were promptly replaced with a new unit and the toy was redesigned, the company behaved in a responsible manner. You don't feel this is a completely honest position and say so. This time you are the only dissenter. The president thanks you for your input, but reiterates the company position.

A month later at a deposition, the plaintiff's attorney asks you directly if you had any prior knowledge of a potential safety defect. What do you answer?

What a pile of issues we have here! We will get to plausible deniability and social responsibility later in the discussion, but initially we will focus on the larger issue, how to answer the question. If you answer "yes," you are articulating your true belief and opening an incredible can of worms. The follow-up questions are sure to put the company in a difficult position. To say the least, this is not a good career move.

You may choose to answer "no" based on the fact that the corporate position is that there was no prior knowledge of a safety defect. That was, after all, the majority opinion. You fulfilled your ethical obligation by voicing your concerns at the time. You are only one person and your reading of the facts may have been wrong. In fact, no one agreed with your interpretation. If you choose this option, you are exercising a common rationalization dodge known as fault dispersal.

Unlike fault reassignment where you attempt to transfer the blame to someone else, fault dispersal is an attempt to hide behind a majority opinion, even if it differs ethically from your own. In other words, a strong personal belief is diluted in a larger mix of contrary beliefs. This is a common practice in professional life. The temptation to go along with a corporate decision is based not only on career concerns, but also on our strong sense of team loyalty. When challenged, we often say, "I told them so," or "I tried to warn them, but was overruled." This is a weak defense. Taken to the extreme it can be used to justify your participation in some pretty questionable activities. Be prepared to ask yourself exactly what you are willing to say or do while hiding behind a majority opinion.

Another variation of fault dispersal is the everybody-does-it excuse. Do you cheat on your taxes, make personal copies on the company machine, or embellish your resume? Sure, everyone does it, right? Even as you offer this defense, you know it is baseless. You wouldn't accept that excuse from your children, so why should you accept it from yourself. When you take this approach, you are not making any attempt to defend your character, but rather admitting that you are as venal as the next guy. That's hardly worth bragging about, now is it? Your mom undoubtedly said something like this: "If everyone else jumped off a bridge, would you?" Score another one for mom!

This argument is also intellectually dishonest. Perhaps it's true that many others, even the majority of others "do it," but not everybody. There are always those ethical few who refuse to be compromised. They chose principle over expediency. Why shouldn't you do the same?

The faulty toy scenario raises two other ethical issues, social responsibility and plausible deniability. If you read the ethical codes published by the established professions, you will find that they all discuss social responsibility, a member's duty to the general public. The underlying theory is that a professional holds a position of public trust and therefore has an obligation to protect the public welfare. For example, engineers and architects may not knowingly approve designs that they know pose a public hazard. They must put their responsibility to the public first. Of course, this responsibility is not limited to engineers and architects. Almost everyone who provides a service or produces a product can have an impact on the general welfare. Those employed by the government either in an elected or professional status have an even greater burden, since they are custodians of public funds and administrators of public programs.

The second issue is that of plausible deniability. For our purposes, we'll define plausible deniability as intentionally restricting our access to information so that we can deny culpability at a later date. It is a legal detour around an ethical problem. This is the I-knew-nothing defense. Turn on your television on any given night and you are sure to hear a politician demonstrating this technique. In the business world, it manifests itself as a reluctance to investigate problems too closely for fear of what might be found. Ignorance may be bliss, but intentional ignorance is unethical.

*   *   *

Men occasionally stumble over the truth, but most of them pick themselves up and hurry off as if nothing ever happened.
                                        ...Winston Churchill

You are the dean of the business school at a major university. You are under pressure from the alumni. They have been openly displeased that the school is consistently in the second tier of business schools as ranked by a leading publication. Displeased alumni mean smaller contributions which mean fewer scholarships to attract the best students, less improvement to facilities and equipment, and the threat of losing faculty to competing institutions. You need to get the ranking into the Top 25.

Faculty diversity has been an issue in past rankings and you have been committed to addressing the problem. In the past year you have made only three faculty hires, two minority males and a female. They represent a 100% increase in both categories. Although still below the national average, it is a step in the right direction and sure to be reflected in the new rankings. The new hires have fit in well and their job performance has been excellent. You are very pleased with your decisions.

One day you get an anonymous email alleging that the new female faculty member's academic credentials are not what she claims them to be. You undertake a very discreet background check and discover that she has not successfully defended her thesis and consequently not completed her doctorate. This is very disturbing, since she represented herself as a Ph.D. during the interview process. The Fall semester is set to begin in three days and the survey for the magazine rankings is due in a month. Other than the sender, you are the only one who knows of the problem.

If you terminate her immediately, your diversity numbers will suffer, and as a consequence, your ranking will be adversely effected. If you keep her on through the survey and terminate her later, you will be perpetrating a fraud on the students and the rest of your faculty, albeit only for a month. You elect to defer the termination in the best interest of the institution. Should the anonymous informant come forward before that, you can always claim an investigation is underway.

Before analyzing this scenario, let's look at another very different one and see if we can see any similarities.

You are the financial officer for the manufacturing division of a computer peripherals company. The head of your division asks you to step into his office and have a seat. His secretary is also present. He gets right to the point.

"As you know, three of our long-time employees have opted for the early retirement package the company has offered. These folks have been loyal and productive employees and we're sure going to miss them. I think we owe them some sort of parting gift to show our appreciation. Unfortunately, there is no budget authority to make this type of purchase. These three are likely to be the first of many to take advantage of this program, so I can't go hitting up the staff for contributions every time this situation comes up and, much as I'd like to, I can't fund this out of my own pocket. Sarah, here, has come up with a solution that I wanted to run by you. She can order an engraved pen and pencil set from our office supplier for about $50 per set. This would come out of her administrative supply budget and, like all expenditures, would require your approval. I just wanted to warn you up front as to what we are planning and to give you the opportunity to object."

You reply that you agree that a parting gift is appropriate and that since Sarah is not asking for additional funds, you would view the purchase of pens and pencils as a legitimate office supply purchase. These funds would have been expended by year's end anyway, so the company is not out anything. It will just require some efficiencies on Sarah's part to make up the difference.

Do you see any similarities in these two cases? Well, for starters, they both involve dishonesty. In the first case it takes the form of withholding information and delaying the required action. That makes you a conspirator in a fraud. In the second case, you are also a conspirator in a fraud by finding a creative way to expend funds in a manner in which you are not authorized. The second commonality is that in both cases the unethical action is rationalized by a method called distortion of the consequences.

In the first case the negative consequences of doing the right thing are magnified to a disastrous proportion. The argument goes like this: if you terminate the faculty member, the diversity numbers and consequently the ranking go down. That keeps the alumni unhappy and their checkbooks closed. Less money means fewer scholarships, less facility and equipment upgrades, and defection of prized faculty. Heck, the apocalypse is upon us!

That's pure nonsense. Sure, there may be some unpleasant consequences, but that doesn't justify unethical behavior. This is a very dangerous approach to ethics. Unfortunately, we see it more and more every day. Political spin masters will manipulate data in a way they know to be untrue. Their rationale is that their opponent is so evil that he must be stopped at any cost. "It would be a disaster for the school board/city council/state/nation if our opponent comes to power." In reality, this is rarely the case. They just want to win and are looking for a rationale to feel good about bad behavior. Similar situations arise regularly in business. We look for justification to sabotage a rival or competitor, so we distort, in our own minds, the consequences of their success.

This is another ethical slippery slope. It is no great leap from distorting consequences, to the Machiavellian "ends-justify-the-means" and from there to "whatever it takes," and finally to complete anarchy. In ethical matters, as in all else, keeping things in the proper perspective is the key.

What of the second case, the retirement gifts? This is also an example of distorting consequences. The difference is that instead of exaggerating them, we minimize them. We convince ourselves that there is no victim or no impact. In this case, the company is not out any money, so where is the harm? The harm is that the conspirators are not acting as good stewards of company resources. Their hearts might be in the right place, but they are still being dishonest and operating outside their authority.

You are not to do evil that good may come of it.
                                                      …Legal maxim

You work for a difficult boss with few people skills. You feel he is two-faced. On one hand he is cooperative and reasonable when dealing with superiors, but on the other hand, demanding and authoritarian when dealing with subordinates. He acts in a ruthless but not dishonest fashion. You don't like him and neither do any of your team members. Much to your chagrin, it appears that he is a rising star in the organization. He gets results and the "big boys" like that. They appear to have no clue as to his methods.

One of your coworkers pulls you aside one day and mentions that he was at a restaurant last night and happened to see the boss at a corner booth with a woman not his wife. They appeared to be "more than friends." He wonders out loud how the company president, a profoundly moral man, would feel about his protégé's extracurricular activities?

"We need to derail this guy," he says. "What do you think about an anonymous note to the old man? This guy treats people like dirt. If he continues to be promoted, he could ruin the company. Besides, he's got it coming."

This case illustrates another variation on the distortion principle, specifically to distort the character of the victim. The more we can convince ourselves that a person is unworthy of ethical treatment, the easier it becomes to treat him or her otherwise. This applies to groups of people as well. For example, during times of war it is routine to demonize the opposition. We characterize them with ethnic stereotypes, focus on their worst atrocities and do whatever else we can to render them sub-human in our own minds. This gives us a free hand to behave as we see fit.

The same thing is true in our professional lives. If we have a competitor, whether that be a personal or corporate rival, it comes in mighty handy if we can convince ourselves that they are evil, despicable and unworthy of ethical treatment. If we can do that, then we feel at liberty to do whatever we deem necessary to stop the villains. They are merely getting what they deserve. After all, what goes around comes around, right?

One problem with this approach is that we have appointed ourselves, perhaps bolstered by prevailing opinion, as judge and jury. In the preceding scenario, we don't have any real proof of our boss' wrongdoing, just some circumstantial evidence. There might be a perfectly innocent explanation. Furthermore, there is no crime and no linkage to the workplace. The fact is that we just don't like this guy and want to get him. Another problem is that unethical behavior is unethical behavior regardless of the character of the victim. In this case, it's just another way of justifying behavior on an ends and means basis.

*   *   *

> *No matter how thin you slice baloney, it's still baloney.*
> ...Alfred E. Smith

> *Advertising is legalized lying.*
> ...H.G. Wells

One of the more popular tools for rationalizing our misbehavior is manipulation of the language. Recently, the relatively obscure verb, to parse, has risen to national prominence in our political dialogue. The actual definition is to break a sentence down into parts, explaining the grammatical form, function and interrelation of each part. It has more recently come to mean to carefully slice a statement so as to be legally accurate, even if untrue. Parsing seems an elegant way to characterize what we common folk would call weasel wording.

Sound ridiculous? Confusing? Here's an example plucked from the headlines and properly sanitized. An adulterous spouse when being deposed is asked if he has ever been alone in a hotel with so-and-so. Since, he can reasonably assume that there were other guests in other rooms as well as hotel staff, he answers, "No, I was never alone with her in a hotel." He is both lying and technically legal.

We come across variations of this phenomenon on a regular basis. As the quotes above indicate, advertisers frequently walk this fine ethical line. Where do you draw the distinction between presenting a product in the most favorable light and deliberate deception? The obvious answer would seem to be intent. If the intent is to deceive, then it is unethical.

Men are more accountable for their motives than for anything else; and primarily, morality consists in the motives.
...Archibald Alexander

You don't have to be a marketing professional to find yourself in this situation. In one way or another we are all involved in some form of advertising, whether promoting a product or service, or claiming a capability, qualification or authority. Furthermore, the practice is not restricted to advertising, as we will see next.

You are the executive assistant to a local stockbroker. Corporate head-quarters has issued a warning on a security widely held by your clients. The warning comes early in the morning as your boss is headed to the airport. He instructs you to call all affected clients and inform them of the warning, "It's extremely important that you speak to each of them personally."

You research the portfolios, identify the affected clients and begin making the calls. You reach most of them, but some are not immediately available, so you leave messages with office staff or voice-mail where possible. Your intention is to follow-up with the people you missed, but a family emergency calls you out of the office and when you return, you are tied up with other client requests.

At 5 PM your boss calls. "Did you speak to all the clients," he asks? "They were all contacted," you reply.

In this case, you don't really want to tell the truth, so you craft an accurate statement with the intent to deceive. Congratulations, you have mastered the art of parsing. In actuality you have misled your boss and deprived some of your clients of the professional service they deserve. You'd never do something like that you say? Let's take a look at your resume.

Most of us want to portray ourselves in the best possible way on our resumes. If we're not careful, this can lead to some embellishment if not outright misrepresentation. How many of us have exaggerated our role or overstated our impact on a program simply by liberal use of the language? If you were a minor contributor on a design team, can you legitimately claim to have "developed" that product? Perhaps you were more modest and just claimed to be "instrumental in the development." Ever exaggerate the number of people you supervised, the extent of your duties, or budget authority, but couched it in terms that were technically accurate? If you answer "no," I suspect you are in the moral minority.

These examples are by no means all-inclusive. There are many other creative ways we can find to skirt principles and act in an expedient manner. They serve only to alert you to the dangers of stretching too far to justify behaviors you know to be unethical.

Chapter Four:
The Long Haul

◆

A man's reputation is what other people think of him; his character is what he really is.

...Jack Miner

Men of genius are admired, men of wealth are envied, men of power are feared; but only men of character are trusted.

...Anonymous

A man's character is his fate.

...Heraclitus

Let's review where we've been. Ethical behavior occurs as a product of a three-step, sequential process. Failure anywhere along this path can lead to unethical behavior. The first step is ethical consciousness, the ability to recognize that you are in a situation that has ethical implications (Chapter1: Sleeping Dogs). Next, you need to make an ethical evaluation, to distinguish between the right and wrong thing to do (Chapter 2:

Twilight Time). Finally, you need to act ethically, to have the courage to do the right thing even if it is not expedient (Chapter3: The Ethical Gymnast).

We also discussed some useful tools for evaluating ethical situations, specifically the *Three Critical Questions*: Who benefits? Who suffers? How would you feel if the situation were reversed? The entire process takes some effort and certainly some self-discipline. So, you might reasonably ask, why bother.

Well, for starters, ethical behavior allows you to feel good about yourself, your standing in your profession and your relationship with society. You like to think of yourself as a good person. That's easier to do if you actually are one. Although we can't assign a dollar amount to this sense of internal and external harmony, we know instinctively that it has value. It is something we would all like to have. The question is what price are we willing to pay to acquire it?

All things being equal, most of us would chose to do the right thing, but things are rarely equal. There are always alternatives to be weighed and choices to be made both in our personal and professional lives. Professionally, we are frequently confronted with an ethical dilemma. Unilaterally do the right thing and watch our rivals gain a competitive advantage or play the game by the same rules they do. Actually, it's not often you against the world. It is more common to find most of your competitors behaving as ethically as you are with only one or two playing outside the rules and realizing an advantage. This doesn't make it any more palatable.

The temptation is to put aside principle in favor of expediency. After all, you have a business or a career to think about. If you take the short-term view expediency seems a sound strategy, but if you take a longer view, you will see that it isn't. As with most things in life, taking a longer perspective is a wiser choice. Many actions that seem favorable in the immediate future can have very unfavorable consequences at a later date.

One of the first things a pilot learns to do during his takeoff run is to transfer his gaze to the end of the runway. If he attempts to steer by looking at the centerline immediately in front of his aircraft, he will have a hard time staying on the pavement. He will be making unnecessary and abrupt control inputs trying to solve a directional problem with too limited a perspective. If, on the other hand, he transfers his attention to the far end of the runway...his goal...he will have a smoother and straighter takeoff run.

You would have the same problem if you tried to speed down the interstate by only observing the lane markers directly in front of your vehicle. You instinctively know you need to look further down the road. The same is true in your ethical decision-making. You need to keep your perspective on the horizon and think long-term. What are your professional goals? Are they to build a successful career or business or to make a one-time killing? Most of us are trying to build something of lasting worth of which we can be proud. The one-time killing is a bank robber's mentality. One big score and he's set (or so he thinks) for life.

Remember that the purpose of professional ethics is to establish harmony in your working environment. This includes relationships with colleagues, clients, peers, superiors, and subordinates. The goal is to create a climate where there is an expectation of behaviors and business practices that fall within established norms. Years of hard won respect can be completely obliterated by one ill-conceived action. You need to consider this when deciding to ignore your ethical standards. It's really all about choices.

The choice is between immediate gratification and long-term success. Is the eventual success of your business or career likely to depend on one decision or one transaction? Probably not. Do you ever again plan to deal with the people who will be the victims of your unethical actions? If so, you had better think long and hard before treating them unfairly. They are certain to remember and react accordingly. I imagine that you remember quite clearly every person who has ever dealt with you in an unethical manner and are loath to deal with him or her again. We spent an entire chapter talking about the lies we tell ourselves to rationalize our actions. Don't think for a minute that they will wash with anybody else. For most of us, the most reliable road to success is to develop lasting professional relationships. That simply isn't possible, if we lose the confidence of the people we deal with.

The choice is between trust and suspicion. Consistent ethical behavior engenders trust, a valuable, but fragile commodity. Often, when time and information are in short supply, you have to go to your reservoir of goodwill to get your clients to stick with you, your colleagues to work with you, your boss to support you, or your team to follow you. "Trust me on this," only works if that trust has been won and sustained. If you have demonstrated in the past that your first interest is self-interest, then you cannot expect people to make that leap of faith. If you have been deceitful or have broken promises, then everything you say and do will be suspect and examined for ulterior motives. Under that kind of scrutiny and mistrust, it will be extremely difficult to get anything done.

The choice is between fairness and selfishness. Do you want to prevail at any cost or on the basis of merit? Is it more important to win than to be fair to all concerned? It's only natural to want to come out on top of a business deal, be promoted, or to close a sale. There is nothing wrong with healthy ambition or being competitive, so long as you play within the rules, not just the statutory rules, but also the ethical rules. To do otherwise is to act selfishly, putting your personal welfare above everyone else's. In the long term, being viewed as a person who plays within the rules means that those who deal with you can have reasonable expectations as to your behavior. That is a core function of professional ethics.

The choice is between openness and concealment. It has been correctly observed that knowledge is power. The question is how will that power be used? Obviously, not every person in every professional relationship needs access to every piece of information. The ethical requirement is to ensure that everyone in the process has access to sufficient data to make an informed decision. Withholding information with the intent of soliciting a decision or action from another party contrary to their own best interests is unethical. Concealing an impending layoff, withholding information on product safety, or failure to disclose conflicts of interest are a few examples. "Let the buyer beware," is a fine proverb and good advice, but it is based on an assumption of ethical failure. Once you have developed a reputation for using information to manipulate behavior, then everything you say will be viewed with skepticism. This is sure to limit your long-term effectiveness.

The choice is between respect and fear. Think of your own professional experiences and then make a list of the people you respect the most? I would guess that among the criteria that you used in making your list were such things as character, integrity and honesty. If asked to make a list of people you least admired, you would probably cite the absence of the same criteria. The problem in the real world is that we can all point to people on the second list who are more successful than those on the first. This doesn't seem right and calls into question the value of ethical standards.

There are exceptions to every rule, but the very fact that they are exceptions makes them stand out. If you combine your two lists in their entirety, my guess is that you will find greater and more consistent success on the ethical side of the ledger. Those who succeed by abandoning their ethics may acquire wealth and power and may be able to intimidate and manipulate, but they are likely more feared than respected.

The choice is between self-esteem and ego. This is the difference between the satisfaction that comes with legitimate accomplishment and the gratification of an immediate desire. One takes time and dedication, the other does not.

* * *

Do not be too moral. You may cheat yourself out of much life. Aim above morality. Be not simply good; be good for something.
                                                    …Henry David Thoreau

Few things are harder to put up with than the annoyance of a good example.
                                                    …Mark Twain

Moral indignation is jealousy with a halo.
                                                    …H.G. Wells

The louder he talked of his honor, the faster we counted our spoons.
                                                    …Ralph Waldo Emerson

It's time for another perspective check. The above quotes serve to illustrate the healthy skepticism most of us have for self-righteousness. While it's good to have a strong moral foundation and to adhere to an ethical code of behavior, it is arrogant and counterproductive to position yourself as a paradigm of virtue and authority on all matters ethical. The immediate problem with this is that we are all human and are all going to occasionally fail. The more we advertise our own virtue, the closer our actions will be scrutinized and the greater the impact of our failure. It is pretty easy to appear a hypocrite in such a situation. Just turn on the television or open a newspaper and you are sure to find some high-profile politician, clergyman or social commentator doing his or her *mea culpa* after being exposed for a fraud. Our reaction is generally one of amusement and satisfaction. My how the mighty have fallen!

This all too frequent scenario leads to public skepticism and facilitates the general decline in societal standards. On a smaller scale, this happens within an organization or profession when the most vocal advocates of ethical standards stumble. If you have staked out the moral high ground, there is no need to trumpet your position. Everyone can see and respect where you stand. By humbly setting the example you will encourage others to do the same.

If you are sincerely interested in promoting professional ethics, the best approach is to become active in your professional associations and your own organizations. If your company does not have a code of ethics, you should work to develop one. If your organization does not have a periodic ethics training program, you should work to establish one. The most practical benefit of periodic ethics training is that it forces everyone to focus, at least for the duration of the training, on the subject. Without a recurring reminder, we all tend to drift off true course. Small, timely corrections make for a smoother journey and avoid larger corrections at a later time.

People behave as their leaders behave, so for an ethics program to be successful it must start at the top. All levels of leadership must walk the walk. If an organization's code of ethics is not the actual standard to which all employees, especially its leaders, are expected to adhere, then it becomes a worthless document and a source of ridicule. If you are in a leadership position, every action you take is observed, analyzed and emulated. If you want an ethical organization, you must lead by example; there is no other choice.

Conclusion

◆

Never try to teach a pig to sing. It wastes your time and annoys the pig.
...Anonymous

Congratulations. If you've come this far, you have invested an hour or so in a subject that can have a significant impact on your professional life. It also demonstrates that you care. Your very willingness to explore the subject indicates that you already aspire to ethical conduct. Unfortunately, those who most need to examine their ethical standards are the least likely to take the time to do so. You can't teach those pigs to sing.

The purpose of this book was not to sit in judgment or to challenge anyone's ethics. It had only one purpose, to get you, the reader, thinking about the subject. The scenarios were designed to demonstrate a small fraction of the ethical situations an individual might likely face in his or her professional life. They were by no means all inclusive. You may disagree with my analysis of the cases. That's fine, at least you thought the scenarios through, considered the circumstances, and formed an opinion.

You opened the musty closet of your conscience and poked around the contents. Perhaps you found some misplaced values or long ignored principles. Perhaps you even awoke the sleeping watchdog that resides there. That would be a good thing. After all, what good is a watchdog that won't bark?

About the Author

◆

George Mazzeo is a retired USAF Colonel. He conducts seminars nationally on professional development subjects to include ethics, leadership, team building, strategic planning, project management and professional communications.

31738697R00068

Made in the USA
San Bernardino, CA
18 March 2016